RAISING GIRLS:
A CHRISTIAN PARENTING BOOK

RAISING GIRLS

A CHRISTIAN PARENTING BOOK

A Practical Guide to
Faith-Based Parenting

TODD JONES

ROCKRIDGE
PRESS

For general information on our other products and services or to obtain technical support, please contact our Customer Care Department within the United States at (866) 744-2665, or outside the United States at (510) 253-0500.

Rockridge Press publishes its books in a variety of electronic and print formats. Some content that appears in print may not be available in electronic books, and vice versa.

Interior Designer: Alan Carr
Cover Designer: Irene Vandervoort
Art Producer: Alyssa Williams
Editor: Mo Mozuch
Production Editor: Ruth Sakata Corley
Production Manager: Jose Olivera

All illustrations used under license from Shutterstock.com and istock.com

Paperback ISBN: 978-1-63807-209-6 | eBook ISBN: 978-1-63807-591-2
R0

*I would like to dedicate this book
to my wonderful, beautiful daughters.
Carly, Cassy, Avery, and Ellie, you
are the sunshine in my world.*

CONTENTS

PART THREE: TARGETED PARENTING STRATEGIES 81

INTRODUCTION

I am so glad you found this book. Being a parent of girls can be among the most amazing, challenging, wonderful, crazy, fun, stressful experiences of your life. Maybe that little bun in the oven is a girl or you're struggling with terrible twos. Maybe she's off to kindergarten and now there are a ton of other influences in her life, or you're staring down adolescence scared out of your mind. Maybe her attitude has soured, or she's all grown up and leaving home and you're wondering what comes next. Wherever you are in your parenting journey, it is my hope that over the next 150 pages or so you will gain insight into God's design and learn some practical tips on how to raise your daughter into the woman God created her to be.

Parenting has never been an easy task. However, I can't help imagining that if 100 years ago someone heard of the challenges we parents face today, their minds would explode. It is no secret that raising godly kids in our current twenty-first-century land-scape is a massive challenge—a culture that doesn't embrace God, the fast pace and stress of our world, and the loud, exces-sive influence of online and social media telling our daughters who they should be, how they should look, and how they should act. Not to mention the busy and overwhelmed lives many par-ents lead. What could go wrong? But God knew that when He decided to give you the blessing of your daughter, and because He believed in you, so do I. You've got this!

As a pastor, speaker, author, and leader working in the church over the last 13 years, I have had a front-row seat to parenting done well and parenting done poorly. Over the years, I have learned so much as I have sat and counseled parents, walked through difficult situations with them and their daughters, and presented biblical principles on parenting. I have witnessed the principles presented in this book lived out, changing lives and hearts on countless occasions. I believe raising kids, daughters specifically, is one of the greatest privileges we will have in this life. But then again, I am very partial; I am no stranger to raising daughters since my wife and I are raising four daughters of our own.

This book's importance cannot be overstated as we navigate raising well-adjusted women who follow Jesus in a time where more challenges and roadblocks exist than ever before. I understand the struggle, and I am living the struggle with you one day at a time. By God's grace and through much prayer and seeking His Word, I am confident we can raise our daughters well. If you are already thinking "raise our daughters well" sounds vague, you're right, it is. There is no cookie-cutter map to tell us exactly how our daughters will turn out or what this parenting journey will be like. So right off the bat, I want you to erase that picture in your mind. Stop comparing yourself to the parent down the street, and focus on becoming the parent God has created you to be.

In this book, you can expect a balance of biblical principles, practical skills, and how-to advice as we dive into a holistic overview of raising girls as Christian parents, exploring foundational parenting principles and specific parenting strategies to solve common issues associated with girlhood. The book is designed to be read start to finish but can certainly be used as a reference guide as you jump to or reread chapters dealing with pertinent issues to your situation.

Wherever you are in your parenting journey, I am positive you will find helpful nuggets for that stage of parenting. However, part 3 is tailored toward the preteen and teenage phases, which may be right where you are—or may offer helpful knowledge to store away and revisit in a few years. So sit back, grab a pen and possibly a notepad or journal if you are the note-taking type, and enjoy the ride.

PART ONE

Raising Girls 101

In this section, you will be provided an overview of Christian parenting principles and an understanding of girls' development into adulthood. Think of this section as the foundation on which to build goals, evaluate values, and incorporate practical advice for specific situations.

1

The Fundamentals of Christian Parenting

The terms "Christian" and "twenty-first century" don't seem to go together. It has become increasingly more difficult to be a Christian, stick to your values, and live a God-honoring life as our world becomes more open and complex. It is no different when it comes to parenting; that's why it is so important we begin with a firm grasp on the fundamentals of Christian parenting.

Parenting Principles from the Bible

The idea of parenting is not something humanity stumbled into by accident; it was created, blessed, and sanctioned by God Himself. Parenting is His idea, and He models it best for us as the perfect Father. We read in 2 Corinthians 6:18, "I will be a Father to you, and you will be my sons and daughters, says the Lord Almighty." This is good news for us. It also means that to truly understand the fundamentals involved in parenting, we must understand God's character and the fruit of His Spirit.

Parenting comes out of an overflow of our personal health and relationship with Jesus. Many people take a "What can I *do* to fix my kid?" approach instead of asking, "Who should I *be* to best parent my kid?" First, let's start with a personal inventory of our spiritual health; it's hard to parent effectively if we are running on empty spiritually, and if we are honest, we may find we often can't parent out of the overflow because there is no overflow to be had. Here are 10 principles I believe are at the core of Christian parenting that form the foundation for how we approach issues throughout this book.

Faith

Parenting should be rooted in your faith in God; however, simply having a religious affiliation is not the full picture of what it means to have faith. God's plan is that we enter into a relationship with Jesus. Accepting His sacrifice is the beginning of our faith and the start of our relationship with Him, but it's just the introduction. Just as when you first met your best friend or your spouse, you probably didn't become close instantly. It is what came *afterward* that developed the friendship. The same goes for our faith relationship. Sometimes people may claim to live a life of faith when all they have done is pray a prayer of introduction. Faith is something that is lived out through seeking God daily, sought after by a firm commitment, wrestled with during difficult times, and continually revisited and renewed.

Grace

Like the song says, grace truly is amazing. It is wild, reckless, and confusing. God's grace doesn't hold back, it isn't cautious in its acceptance and love, and the truth behind it doesn't always make sense to our human brains. In contrast, the scales of justice are not a concept that needs to be explained to anyone; we are wired with a predisposition to keep score, earn, and try to prove ourselves to God. But grace is the love God shows to the unlovely, the peace of God given to the restless, the unmerited favor of God.

Joseph R. Cooke said, "Grace is the face that love wears when it meets imperfection." It is easy to forget that our kids are just kids (even when they're teenagers) and they *will* mess up.

They are not perfect, but neither are we, and we all deserve grace. As parents, we must learn to give ourselves and our daughters grace.

Mercy

The Oxford English Dictionary defines mercy as "compassion or forgiveness shown toward someone whom it is within one's power to punish or harm."

Parenting is a lifelong mission of mercy. Think of it this way: We are called to be God's first responders. A first responder sees a great need and does what it takes to meet that need. They are not there to judge, criticize, or give a lecture on how you got yourself into the mess. Yes, you want your children to be aware of how they got into a bad situation in the hopes they can avoid it in the future, but you want to rescue them with forgiveness, love, and mercy. When your children need help, rush to them with the power and beauty of God's mercy.

As Luke 6:36 says, "Be merciful, just as your Father is merciful."

Hope

As Christians, we have a hope that is only found in Jesus. John 16:33 says, "In this world you will have trouble. But take heart! I have overcome the world." Our hope is found in the fact that through faith we have been saved by grace. Life is going to chew us up and spit us out sometimes, but the fact is, Jesus died for us, He loves us, and He will never forsake us. That is where our hope is found. Parenting can feel hopeless, whether it is the fourth night of no sleep because your infant won't take the bottle or the fourth night of your teenager missing their curfew, but let's remind ourselves that our hope—and our daughters' hope—isn't in our current parenting situation; rather, it is in Jesus.

Joy

Philippians 4:4 says, "Rejoice in the Lord always. I will say it again: Rejoice!"

Easier said than done! Parenting is hard. There will likely be times when nothing goes as planned. Perhaps your daughter has a meltdown in the middle of the movie theater, loses her clarinet on the day of the concert, or decides the new clothes she picked out last week simply will not do for family pictures and you just want to pull your hair out. It may seem impossible to be happy during those times. But that is exactly when we need to distinguish between joy and happiness. Happiness is often based on our external circumstances, whereas joy is something we choose to produce. Joy is not a product of our surroundings, success, or fulfilled wish list. It is sourced internally by an eternal hope that comes from our relationship with Jesus.

Romans 15:13 tells us, "May the God of hope fill you with all joy and peace as you trust in him." Our joy should not be founded in our circumstances but rather our relationship with Jesus. Jesus is our source of joy.

Humility

"I messed up. I am sorry." These are six of the hardest, most important words you will ever utter as a parent. Humility is not a natural inclination for us as humans, which is probably why it is talked about so much in scripture. James 4:10 tells us, "Humble yourselves before the Lord, and He will lift you up," and Philippians 2:3 says, "Do nothing out of selfish ambition or vain conceit. Rather, in humility value others above yourselves."

Humility is one of the best parenting tools available. Admit when you are wrong, don't know the answer, or need to ask for help. The times when I have gotten closest with my daughters are not when I held on to what I "knew" was right but when I was able to sit down and tell them I was wrong.

Steadfastness

First Corinthians 15:58 says, "Therefore, my dear brothers and sisters, stand firm. Let nothing move you. Always give yourselves fully to the work of the Lord, because you know that your labor in the Lord is not in vain."

In all aspects of our life and faith, it can be tempting at times to wave the white flag. Life is difficult, and serving God can be even more difficult, especially when we're going through trials like financial struggles, professional disappointments, frustrating relationships, or conflicts with our kids. But this is where the idea of steadfastness comes in. Yes, we should be steadfast in our faith, but just as much in our parenting.

There may be days when we do not want to parent, follow God's principles in parenting, or even get out of bed. But a continued commitment to the truth and instilling the truth in our children should be a reminder that is on repeat in our brains and gives us the desire to never give up.

Authenticity

It is easy to fall into the trap of putting on a mask. I have been guilty of this more times than I care to admit. I was recently at the store with my daughters and ran into a guy I had played softball with briefly a couple of years prior. We began chatting, and I realized I started talking differently, saying things about mutual acquaintances that I would never say in other situations, and just flat-out making things up to impress this guy. I shook off the feeling, we left, and it was fine, no big deal.

I had forgotten two things: First, God created me to be me, not someone else. Second, my kids were watching me. In an instant, they saw me put on a mask, be inauthentic, and become someone other than who God created me to be. Authenticity matters.

We will return to this principle continually throughout this book because it is so crucial to growing as a person and a parent.

Understanding God's Love

We have all heard the phrase "God loves you," but as any parent can tell you, there is a difference between hearing something and understanding it. God's love, like His grace, is consistent, persistent, vast, generous, and unconditional no matter how far we run or how many times we turn our back on Him. We like to throw the word *love* around often, but this love is not the type we have for our favorite dinner or amusement park. God's love is mind-blowing.

But His love goes beyond just its characteristics, as the Bible says in 1 John 4:7–8: "Dear friends, let us love one another, for love comes from God. Everyone who loves has been born of God and knows God. Whoever does not love does not know God, because God is love." God's love is not something He does, it is who He is, which means if we are going to practice love toward others, we must know God, or we cannot understand love.

Prayer

Christian writer Max Lucado has said, "Our prayers may be awkward. Our attempts may be feeble. But since the power of prayer is in the one who hears it and not in the one who says it, our prayers do make a difference." Prayer is like plugging into God's power source. I can't count all the times I have felt powerless when it comes to parenting. I have felt overwhelmed, unequipped, burned out, at the end of my rope, and just plain not good enough. In those moments, I remind myself that God is enough. We have open access to God through prayer—why not use this amazing resource often?

A NUANCED PERSPECTIVE ON AUTHORITY AND DISCIPLINE

Our guide as Christians and as parents is scripture. We look to God's Word to guide us and help us when it comes to raising our children. However, many times we allow tradition to overshadow the heart of God's Word.

The Bible dictates that parents have God-given authority over their children (Ephesians 6:1, Colossians 3:20), and this is true. Some "traditional" methods of parenting interpret authority to mean authoritarian. However, the authority we see in scripture is a lot more *authoritative* than authoritarian. Both authoritative and authoritarian parents hold very high standards for their kids' behavior, but they play out in very different ways. Authoritarian parents impose tight psychological control over their kids, utilize a sense of fear in their kids, and behave as if they are always right and their kids need to always accept their judgment "because they said so," while authoritative parents discuss and explain rules, teach their kids to think critically, empower them to make choices, and behave warmly toward their children.

The clearest example of this authoritative approach is seen from Jesus and His ministry as He talks about love and serving (John 8:1–11, 13:15, 15:15). In short, we must ask ourselves if our authority is rooted in love or power and position.

Our understanding of this concept of authority spills over to how we carry out discipline. Are we practicing positive discipline that seeks to help children learn and make connections between their behavior/actions and their impact on others or punitive discipline designed to control or regulate a child's behavior through fear?

We will discuss this in greater detail in part 2, but we need to remember parenting can be an expression of worship. How are you worshipping God through your authority?

What It Means to Be a Christian Parent Today

In the past, when it came to Christian parenting, there was a large emphasis on outward appearance. If you were able to look and act the right way in public, sitting still in church and looking adults in the eye when you spoke to them, you were thought to be on the right Christian path, a good kid with excellent parents. If you had extreme hair, wild clothing choices, or multiple piercings, you were probably perceived as rebellious or irresponsible.

While there's something to be said for kids behaving well in public (especially when they're little), we have learned our focus as parents should be more on the heart and less on outward appearance. In other words, parenting is not about behavior modification in our kids but rather heart adaptation—when their good behavior comes from a loving, Christlike heart. This happens when we make the shift from religion being our guide to our relationship with Jesus being our guide. Our priority as parents is for our kids to see the real Jesus and have a real relationship with Him, even if we disagree with their clothing choices or they have a meltdown at the grocery store. When this is our priority, we can live and parent accordingly.

Christian Parents Are Shepherds

The analogy of a shepherd probably won't be lost on any of Christ's followers, since that is what Jesus is for us: a good shepherd. But what does a shepherd actually do? Their primary responsibility is the safety and welfare of the flock. They are a guard, guide, physician, and provider. Shepherds are self-sacrificing.

As Christian parents, we need to ask ourselves: What does it look like to shepherd our daughters? Obviously, we aren't going to carry a staff and follow them around making sure they don't fall off a cliff, right? (Well, maybe sometimes.) But our calling to be shepherds means truly knowing our children personally and intimately. It means loving our children, desiring what's best for them, wanting God's will and purpose for their life rather than our own, and laying down our comfort in ordinary moments to prioritize them. It means leading them to Jesus and providing for their spiritual needs by helping them know God's Word, praying with them, and getting them involved in God's church.

Christian Parents Serve as Vessels for God's Will

I have a good friend who is a tattoo artist. He is very skilled at what he does and uses his time and talents to make a difference for people. Recognizing the gift God gave him, he made the decision to use his skills to help people find hope in Jesus. It is not uncommon for him to pray with people, sharing Jesus with them and even leading them to become Christians, all while he's tattooing them. My friend recognized God had given him an opportunity to be a vessel for His will and took that opportunity, so much so that his tattoo shop is named Vessel Tattoo Co.

As parents, we can see what is in front of us as an opportunity to serve God and be a vessel for Him. As Ezekiel 36:27 says, "I will put my Spirit in you and move you to follow my decrees and be careful to keep my laws." Parenting is an opportunity to let the Spirit move us so we can point our daughters to Jesus and equip them to follow Him on their own.

Christian Parents Reflect God's Love

God's love is unconditional, deeper, and more merciful than any other love. I remember when I was nine, being corrected by my mom for something undoubtedly very selfish I had done. I don't recall what I did, but I do recall responding to my mom's "I still love you" with "What if I don't love you?" At that moment, there were probably 100 un-Christlike things my mom wanted to say to me, but she softly replied, "My love for you is not dependent on your love for me."

God's love is a self-sacrificing, unconditional, do-whatever-it-takes type of love that is counter to the anger and resentment we may sometimes feel—what our flesh may want us to give into. When our daughters are ungrateful, selfish, lashing out, breaking curfew, or dating someone we can't stand, we must remember and reflect God's love, not our human love.

Christian Parents Push for Authenticity

I would rather my kids be real than right. I remember once over-hearing my daughter tell her friend a lie in the back seat to sound cooler than she was. Later, when I asked her about it, it led to her confessing she lied at school all the time about the size of our house, places she had traveled, people she had met, and anything else that might impress her peers. My heart broke because I could relate. Growing up, when I knew something wouldn't paint me in the perfect light, I would just wear a mask to get the recognition I desired. It wasn't until I was in college—when I attended a church that was all about being real with ourselves, God, and others—that I truly understood God's grace.

To truly understand Jesus and all He offers, we need to be authentic. As parents, we can cultivate a culture of authenticity by focusing on relationship, listening to our daughters with the sole purpose of understanding, expressing feelings, and leading the way by being authentic ourselves. In anything, modeling is the best form of teaching, and it is even more true with authenticity. Be honest; be real.

The Challenges Christian Parents Face Today

As if we haven't said it enough already, parenting is tough. Living as a Christian is also tough. In John 16:33, Jesus Himself says, "In this world you will have trouble." There are many challenges existing now that past generations didn't necessarily worry about. The world's preference for moral relativism over God's truth, Christian principles being devalued in society, graphic violence and casual sexuality in movies and video games, and a generally negative view of religion are just a few examples of how culture has changed in my lifetime.

The number of influences and voices shaping girls in particular has increased exponentially. Even our best attempts to shelter and protect them from harmful or unsavory influences is circumvented by their access to technology, the internet, and social media. Looking at airbrushed images of models and influencers, girls are especially susceptible, even at young ages, to developing a hyperfocus on appearance, which can lead to troubled self-esteem and depression.

The Ubiquity of the Internet and Social Media

We can't escape it: the internet and social media are everywhere! There are many, many wonderful things the internet has brought us, and I am not just talking about funny cat videos. But it has also introduced an entirely new problem when it comes to seeing our worth and value.

Twenty years ago, a girl might have one or two girls in her class that she deemed prettier or more successful than herself and would compare herself to. Now, after 30 seconds of scrolling through someone's filtered and edited social media feed, our daughters can feel about an inch tall. Girls are bombarded with a false cultural standard they cannot possibly live up to, and they cannot escape it—it is literally in their hands.

All of us, but especially our daughters, need to understand love over likes and value over views. Social media has set up a visible ranking of our "desirability" that anyone can see. *How many likes did I get? How many views do I have? How much significance do I hold?*

The truth is we don't have to do anything to earn our worth and value. It was already assigned to us by God: "For you created my inmost being; you knit me together in my mother's womb. I praise you because I am fearfully and wonderfully made" (Psalm 139:13–14). Our value was also proved: "But God demonstrates his own love for us in this: While we were still sinners, Christ died for us" (Romans 5:8).

Don't worry, we will talk more about navigating the internet and social media in a later chapter (see page 120). For now, let's consider it one of several challenges we must face while raising daughters.

A General Decline in Religiosity

According to a Gallup research study on religion, over the past two decades, the percentage of Americans who do not identify with any religion has grown from 8 percent between 1998 and 2000 to 13 percent between 2008 and 2010 to 21 percent over the past three years. However, we don't need research or statistics for us to know that our culture is bending away from God. The difficulty for us as Christian parents lies in the fact that our culture embraces values that may be at odds with our own.

We are raising our daughters in a culture that increasingly challenges our value systems. Things we consider crass, rude, unethical, or morally wrong may be celebrated by people our daughters admire. This is one of the largest challenges when it comes to raising our kids as Christians. Again, Jesus never said it would be easy. But take heart—it isn't impossible, especially with God as our guide. We will talk more in chapter 3 about defining and instilling values in our daughters.

We Live in a Magnifying Glass Society

Thanks to the internet, social media, and the judgmental nature of our culture, it can feel like every move we make as parents is under a magnifying glass. Maybe you have experienced a DM from a parent because your kid's clothes didn't match or you let your child watch a movie that someone else deems inappropriate. Maybe you tried to join a parenting group, only to have other parents tell you how their ideas about sleep training, bottle use, bedtime routine, or discipline habits are better than yours. Whether it's your children's diet, screen-time schedules, behavior (especially for kids who are neuroatypical), or choice of friends, it can seem like your in-laws, friends, neighbors, or church members just can't wait to point out all your mistakes. Parent judging comes in all different shapes and sizes, but it always makes our job more difficult.

And the criticism doesn't just come from outside sources. Maybe you have found a trending list of dos and don'ts online that only made you more aware of how lacking you are in a certain area or feel you're failing at parenting in general. We fight for our daughters to not get caught up in peer pressure or insecurity, but it is just as dangerous of a trap for us as well.

As parents, we need to know who we are and be secure in who we are. We need to remember who we serve and that our God's opinion is way more important than the opinions of others. Our true north is in God and His Word, not some random internet commentator—though it's helpful to be open to different points of view, as He can speak through others as well. It's a difficult balance.

Traditional Expectations

Past generations held certain stereotypical expectations of what a Christian parent was. While some things were valuable, such as placing a high level of importance on scripture, a commitment to attending the local church, and a strong work ethic, many other things—like corporal punishment or putting appearances first—were not. We have the challenge of breaking away from what was done while keeping what truly matters.

I enjoy cooking. My interest started when my wife and I got one of those boxed meal subscriptions that gets delivered with a recipe and all the ingredients. I discovered that I could change recipes to better fit me and the needs of my family. I didn't have to do it the way it had been done in the past just because that's how they did it. However, what was required was sticking to the main things. I couldn't decide to throw out the patty, bun, and cheese and still call it a cheeseburger; it would just be a weird salad. There are some essentials I need, but I also have freedom to switch it up.

The same goes for parenting. Maybe you grew up in a church that said children were to be seen and not heard. While the principle still applies to behaving well in church, you realize kids can learn by serving, teaching others, and having conversations. Or perhaps your parents followed traditional gender roles where your mom cooked and your dad fixed stuff, but now you understand it doesn't matter who does what as long as the principles of serving and helping each other are followed. We do not have to be tied to how things were done in the past, how we were raised, or our own stereotypical beliefs about what a Christian parent should be. Tradition is not our guide; Jesus and the Word of God are. We have freedom to break away from what was if we stick to what truly matters and keep Jesus at the heart of our parenting.

Raising a Christian Child
in a Secular Society

Like it or not, we're living in the twenty-first century. It doesn't matter how much we might wish for a time machine, we still must navigate raising a Christian child in a secular society. So how do we do it?

Ultimately, even for Christian parents, how you raise your children is your choice. I have seen parents who don't feel comfortable involving their kids in any secular activity, even sports, while some parents are fine with their kids participating in unchaperoned dances, parties, or R-rated movies. There really isn't a "right" way to navigate this. However, there is a biblical lens and a set of questions we should be asking as Christian parents.

In John 17:14–16, we see Jesus praying for his followers. He says, "I have given them your word and the world has hated them, for they are not of the world any more than I am of the world. My prayer is not that you take them out of the world but that you protect them from the evil one. They are not of the world, even as I am not of it."

In short, we are called to be *in the world*, not *of the world*, meaning we have been placed in this world, and not by accident—we are exactly where God wants us to be. As Christians, we should be thermostats that set the temperature instead of thermometers that merely reflect the temperature around us.

Here are five questions to process what areas you may be more flexible in allowing your child to participate and what areas you will choose to be stricter:

1. How firm is my child's identity, and will they allow this influence to override who they are?

2. Will my child be able to be a thermostat or a thermometer in this environment?

3. What good can my child bring to this environment without it having the opposite effect?

4. Am I able to have open dialogue with my child about the environment they're in and how it aligns or doesn't align with our beliefs?

5. Have I done my part to prepare my child for this environment and the possible influences they will encounter?

Again, it is your decision how much or how little you want to allow your daughter to be involved in culture and the world around her. Whatever your decision is, make sure Jesus is at the core, not fear, lack of care, peer pressure, tradition, or anything else.

One of my daughters recently got invited to a sleepover. My wife and I looked at the lack of supervision, strong influences, and my daughter's propensity for people-pleasing and decided she would not be allowed to go. As we delivered the disappointing news, we laid out our reasons and used the situation to talk to her about not putting herself in situations where it would be difficult to do the right thing. We discussed the values that drove our decision and the importance they should play in our lives. She was disappointed, but she eventually understood the *why*.

As you finalize your decision, make sure you have open dialogue with your daughter instead of falling back on "because I said so." Remember, the heart is what matters. It is not about doing or not doing a certain activity. We need to use the situation in front of us as a springboard for a conversation to target the heart.

What's more, the decisions you make don't have to be permanent. Be open, try new things, continually learn, and seek help from other parents. Don't judge another parent if their decision is different from yours. The culture we live in is overwhelming, but the God we serve is bigger than our culture.

2

From Girls to Women: Understanding Your Daughter's Development

As parents, we know our daughters change often, but we don't always understand what's happening, which can be frustrating. In this chapter, we'll discuss a general overview of a girl's development spiritually, emotionally, socially, physically, and sexually as they transition into their teenage years and, eventually, adulthood.

Influence Is Everything

Nature or nurture? The answer is "yes." Both are major contributing factors to how your daughter will learn, grow, and develop. There are things we as parents can control and influence, but there are also factors, such as hormones, that are out of our control. These require just as much patience and understanding, not just from us but from our daughters who are going through those changes.

However, taking time to think through the influences we do have some control over, and understanding how they can shape our daughter's development, is extremely important. It is no secret the influences around us guide and shape who we become.

1 Corinthians 15:33: "Do not be misled: 'Bad company corrupts good character.'"

Proverbs 27:17: "As iron sharpens iron, so one person sharpens another."

Proverbs 13:20: "Walk with the wise and become wise, for a companion of fools suffers harm."

We could go on and on with verses on this subject. While these verses speak specifically to friends, they can also apply to all areas of influence. These are some key areas to consider when thinking about who and what influences your daughter.

Her Family History and Structure

Life is busy, so we may not think much about how our family history and structure affect our daughters' long-term development. We should. I bet if you take a moment to reflect on your own life, you could point out how family history and structure impacted your development.

Here is why: Humans rely heavily on observation and learning for their development. We are not born knowing how to behave in society, and therefore we learn behaviors from the environment around us. By default, the family becomes the main environment by which these behaviors are learned. Not only does family health history play a role in development, especially if there is some type of developmental disorder or health concern that makes development in some area a challenge, but factors such as parental marital statuses, financial situations, household stresses, plurality of caregivers, and transitions in family structures have a major impact on the development of a child into adulthood.

Her Family Values

History and structure, while partially within our control, some-times simply happen to our children instead of us intentionally creating them. Family values, on the other hand, allow us to have more of an active role. The values we create in our households have a massive effect on the environment our kids are raised in and influenced by.

The importance of values cannot be overstated. They provide protection, guidance, affection, and support for our daughters. Instilling family values can protect and guide children against making hurtful decisions in the future as they teach a sense of right and wrong. For example, if a value like respect is not present in the family—if concerns are dismissed or family members talk down to one another—it becomes a part of the development process and plays out by your daughter acting out in the same disrespectful ways toward others in her life.

As parents, we have an opportunity to set those values, model them, and instill them in our daughters throughout every developmental stage. The application of the values will change as she grows, develops, and encounters new situations, but the presence of the values in her life remains crucial.

Her Community

"Show me your friends, and I will show you your future." Who knows who originally said it (every grandparent everywhere?), but this quote is so true. If we define "community" as simply the people our daughters spend time with, we have a window into one of the major influences on their behavior and development. Sometimes, depending on our daughter's age, an outside influ-ence is even greater than our own.

As I think back on my life, I can clearly point out the reasons I talked the way I did, laughed at what I laughed at, and chose the activities I did, and those reasons had names—they were friends, family, and others I interacted with on a regular basis. Your child is likely influenced in the same ways. As parents, we need to be aware of these influences and the effect they can have on our daughters. Part of this is teaching them to stay true to their values regardless of influences around them, but another part is making sure their communities are pushing them toward positive behavior.

Get to know your daughter's friends. Sit down with her when she comes home from hanging out, and talk to her about the people she spends time with. Open your home to her friends, and make it a comfortable place for them to gather. Perhaps schedule a weekly breakfast or late-night ice cream outing to ask her questions about what her friends are like. Like almost every aspect of parenting, her community is another opportunity to open lines of communication and help talk her through why it matters.

Her Faith Community

There are multiple factors in the development of your child when it comes to church and faith. Church offers social connections/ influences, moral development as your child is beginning to set their moral compass, biblical knowledge, and hopefully a springboard to a relationship with Jesus that will continue to grow and develop as they do.

Depending on their level of involvement, the church can help bring a sense of belonging and security to your daughter's life. I've been involved in ministry in the church for the last decade and a half, and I have seen many students blossom in their knowledge, maturity, and social development thanks to their time with us. I remember a young lady named Katie walking into youth group for the first time. She was scared, sat in the back, and barely talked to anyone. As group was about to start, I noticed a leader introducing herself and sitting with Katie. She began to build a relationship with not only that leader but other students, growing in her knowledge and faith and developing into a leader herself. She continued to get more involved and joined the student leadership team. She became one of the strongest students I've ever seen spiritually, socially, and emotionally. She possessed incredible potential on her own, but her involvement in the church helped her discover it.

Her Interests

Sports, dance, choir, band, gymnastics, theater, art—the list goes on. These activities can all have a major impact on your daughter's development. My wife grew up playing soccer and can point out so many aspects of it that helped her grow and develop. Physically, she had to understand her body and how it needed to move in order to produce the best results. Mentally, she had to stretch herself to deeply understand how the game worked and the type of thinking required to stay alert. Emotionally, she had to learn to handle failure, competition, overcoming adversity, controlling her frustration, and much more. Socially, she was forced to learn how to interact with different types of people in a variety of situations within the team.

Whatever the activity, the amount of time, dedication, and long-term commitment can have a massive impact on your daughter's development. Try to identify and steer her toward positive interests when she is young. Expose her early, teach her, and talk about the positive qualities it will foster. Help her pursue her interests by making time for them, finding opportunities for her to practice them, and cheering her on when she is discouraged.

Spiritual Development

As kids learn and grow mentally and physically, they also grow spiritually. If a child is raised in a Christian household, their spiritual development should be part of this growth as well. As they get smarter and more mature, the hope is that their spiritual selves will, too.

Jesus Himself recognized the importance of understanding like a child: "And he said: 'Truly I tell you, unless you change and become like little children, you will never enter the kingdom of heaven'" (Matthew 18:3). Kids have a unique opportunity to see the gospel as it was intended, but our hope is that they continue to grow in their faith. This was Paul's hope as well, as he wrote in 1 Corinthians 13:11, "When I was a child, I talked like a child, I thought like a child, I reasoned like a child. When I became a man, I put the ways of childhood behind me."

My wife and I have been Christians almost our whole lives, which means our daughters are growing up in a Christian household. They started hearing about Jesus before they could talk. We would talk about Jesus often, tell Bible stories, and read the kids' Bible with the big cartoon pictures as a part of our everyday life. All my kids have attended church their entire lives, and my oldest (twin) daughters prayed the salvation prayer at the age of four. They didn't fully understand it all, but they followed what they could at whatever level they were at. Not only did they see us model Christianity as we served in the church, but we also got them involved as well. They were seven years old when they first started helping with our church's food distribution ministry. They would wake up early every Saturday morning and stuff boxes with food, and we would deliver them to needy families. As we drove, we would talk about the heart behind why we served others. The conversation about God stayed open as they got older, and the level of their questions increased; they could ask us anything. My prayer for all of my daughters is that they continue to grow and learn at every stage, whether at church or at home.

Development happens at different stages. Our job as parents is to continue to put our children in places where they can learn and experience God. But what if your child, or children, doesn't want to be a part of the church or believe in God?

One of the best things we can do as parents is love our kids regardless of where they are in their faith journey. Love is what compels people, not judgment or rules. We can also model it.

One of the biggest reasons kids walk away from faith when they get older is because they never saw it modeled in their home; it was a show on Sunday and not genuine the other six days.

Emotional Development

Do you like roller coasters? Because that's exactly what life can feel like with our daughter some days. She wakes up mad because she's tired, but she overslept at the same time. Then she is super happy because you made her favorite breakfast, but then she remembers her BFF is on vacation and she won't see her at school and is very sad again. Then she realizes she has art class today and is happy again, until she remembers that boy she is interested in sits across from her and she is instantly dealing with anxiety.

There are a lot of developmental changes that happen within our daughters, but emotional development may be the hardest and most critical to navigate with empathy and support, especially between the ages of 8 and 12, when they're moving toward puberty and adulthood. Let's take a look at a few of the most common issues for emotional development and the challenges they bring.

Mood Swings

From dealing with change and pressure, to struggling with identity and self-image, to trying to figure out biology and why their body is doing what it's doing, it is easy to see why your daughter might experience mood swings. But understanding why mood swings happen doesn't help navigate it, so here are a few tips to keep things positive:

Keep your cool. Raising your voice or rolling your eyes back at your daughter—as frustrated as you may be—is counterproductive and likely to escalate issues.

Encourage healthy sleep habits and establish an exercise routine. Exercise is a natural mood booster, and a lack of sleep can increase difficulty regulating emotions.

Support a healthy diet. Eating breakfast, reducing caffeine, and decreasing sugar are just a few things that can help your daughter feel more balanced.

Be consistent. Whether it is routine, discipline, or words of encouragement, not giving up and staying consistent will build her sense of security.

Keep the communication open. Try to stay connected to your daughter, even when her behavior is difficult to manage. Finally, *have patience.* This, too, will pass.

Impulsiveness

"Think before you act!" is a phrase that has made or will make it out of your mouth before your parenting journey concludes. Most kids (and most adults) have moments when they are impulsive and do things before they can stop themselves. It happens to everyone. But when impulsive behavior—like blurting out, engaging in something dangerous without considering consequences, or becoming violent and aggressive—persists or becomes a pattern, it may be a sign of self-control issues. It could be caused by a lack of maturity for their age, lack of sleep, stress, frustration dealing with a difficult situation, or ADHD or mood disorders.

What can we do? If impulsiveness occurs frequently, take notes and track your daughter's behavior to know when and why it's happening. Talk to teachers and health care providers to get their input and advice. Have conversations with your daughter about self-control, and try to discover the "why" behind her behavior rather than just correcting her surface-level behavior.

Confidence Lapses

As our daughters develop emotionally, one of the biggest up-and-down aspects can be their level of confidence. Your daughter's confidence can be affected by body image, friends or lack of friends, parental support, stressful life events such as divorce or moving houses, poor performance at school, unrealistic goals, or rude comments or comments taken the wrong way. She will constantly be bombarded by situations that can shake her.

These lapses in confidence can manifest in both mood swings and impulsiveness, but they can also have other social and emotional consequences. Your daughter might struggle with relationship troubles or difficulty making friends; avoiding new things and not taking opportunities; feeling unloved and unwanted; low levels of motivation; anxiety; depression; or negative coping mechanisms such as earlier sexual activity, drinking, or drugs.

I am not trying to scare you or jump to the worst-case scenario. Confidence lapses will happen to almost every kid, but that doesn't mean your daughter is destined for trouble. Still, watching out for the signs listed above can guide you in helping your daughter navigate these trials.

You can help by talking about the difficulties she is facing. Speak her language. Especially in her teen years, she may be more comfortable opening up over a text message conversation instead of talking face-to-face. Constantly remind her of where her worth and value come from. They come from Jesus, not her achievements or appearance. Be real and discuss your struggles and issues in the past. Share with her how you overcame them or wish you would have dealt with them.

Defining Themselves

People are constantly on a search for belonging and understanding of self, especially in the preteen and teen years. A major part of emotional development is figuring out how to define oneself in terms of values, beliefs, and role in the world. Identity formation means developing a strong sense of self, personality, connection to others, and individuality. It is a vital part of shaping your daughter's perception of belonging, not just in her preteen and teen years but for the rest of her life.

I have seen this play out in ways like girls completely switching friend groups, going from wearing colorful clothing to only wearing black, or becoming obsessively involved in their sport or activity. One girl in my ministry who was athletic began defining herself by her workouts and started workout-themed social media accounts. Another girl became obsessed with the color orange and wore only orange as a way of gaining attention and standing out.

Unhealthy ways of trying to define themselves can include seeking status symbols such as clothing and possessions to create a sense of positive affiliation, rebellion, cliques, or identifying with a famous person and trying to become like that person.

As our daughters start to define themselves, we can model a healthy self-identity, avoid comparing our kids with others, give them compliments and positive reinforcements, communicate love for them, and, most importantly, remind them their identity is in Jesus. Again, we will talk more about this in chapters 9 and 14.

DEPRESSION AND ANXIETY

Depression and anxiety. These are two very common but potentially very scary words for parents.

In a study published by the journal **Translational Psychiatry** in 2017, more than one-third of teenage girls in the United States experience a first episode of depression (almost three times the rate for boys). The National Survey of Drug Use and Health also did a study between 2009 and 2014 that showed 36.1 percent of girls reported depression, compared to 13.6 percent of boys. We also know those numbers have increased dramatically in recent years. Why is this so?

Emotional, cognitive, and social-interpersonal changes due to puberty are just a few of the main reasons why tween and teenage girls are at such a high risk. The tremendous social pressure girls experience can lead to lack of confidence and self-esteem and become a prime environment for anxiety and depression. Mental health conditions, learning disabilities, ongoing/chronic pain, or having been the victim or witness of violence can also be risk factors. Social media in particular can be detrimental to a girl's mental health, as it can lead to body image issues and become an outlet for bullying. Monitor your daughter's activity for trends in this direction, and if her mental health seems to be worsening with increased exposure, consider restricting her social media use.

It is critically important that we make time to have conversations with our daughters, actively listen to them and their feelings, and notice when things change in their demeanor and regular routines. Pray for your daughter often. Realize you and she can't do life alone, and get other positive influences involved in her life. Spend time talking with her and teaching her about the importance of looking to Christ in difficult times. As parents, we also need to realize when our daughter needs help outside of our capabilities. There may be times when professional help is needed and should be sought out.

Social Development

Every aspect of development is linked together in some way, and it is no different with social development. Emotional, spiritual, and physical development all play a role in your daughter's social development as she transitions into adolescence and adulthood.

The adolescent social scene can be a difficult one to navigate, especially with the opportunity for instant communication and comparison through social media. So much of your daughter's self-worth is tied to her social life. It can be tricky when our children start shifting away from us as their primary social connection, but that connection is vital as we help them navigate the social changes in their lives. Remember, parents tend to influence long-term decisions, such as career choices, values, and morals, while friends are more likely to influence short-term choices, such as appearance and interests.

Influences are a massive part of shaping our daughters' social worlds, but there are some significant and common social changes that also play a role.

Friendships in Flux

In early elementary school, my daughter came home one day and announced she had met a new best friend. This was not a shock, considering she had made the same announcement three times previously in the last two weeks. When I asked her what qualifications this person had to be her best friend, I had to smile at the simplicity of what it took. She was going down the same slide on the playground, her favorite color was pink, and she was willing to play tag. Why wouldn't they be best friends?

This is exactly what many elementary- and younger-age friendships are built upon as well as parents being friends or simply seeing that person regularly. However, this changes as our daughters begin to develop emotionally and socially. The choice of who they hang out with starts being shaped by common interests, social pecking order, level of maturity, appearance, developing personalities, sense of humor, and more. While our daughters (and everyone around them) are in the process of discovering themselves, it may mean a shift or multiple shifts in friend groups. In contrast to adult friendships, which generally don't shift often, friendship shifts can be a frequent occurrence during adolescence.

A Growing Desire for Privacy

I remember shrugging and giving a confused sideways glance at my wife the first time my oldest daughter headed straight to her room and closed the door. After checking with her to make sure everything was okay, I was even more confused and surprised that she *was* okay; she just wanted her own space. It feels weird to us, but it is exactly what happens as our daughters start to develop socially.

It can be a shock when our daughters, who normally tell us every detail of their day, stop telling us all about their conversations and begin processing emotions on their own and desiring privacy. It becomes especially tricky when their desire for privacy with the phone, the one you pay for and know the dangers of, becomes a priority for them.

Does this mean we completely draw back and just let them do their thing? No. We need to balance giving them space with being there for them and staying involved in what matters. We might get involved in things that are character shaping, like who they date or their friend choices, or major decisions like quitting a sports team, as opposed to just allowing them space to process their day, do their homework, or make their dinner that night.

Independence

"No! I do it myself!" You probably heard this a lot when your daughter was a toddler. At this age, your child is starting to feel the need for independence, but she still needs you for so many things. You might do things like letting her buckle her car seat, only to buckle it correctly five seconds later, or allow her to fill her own sippy cup from the water dispenser in the fridge and then clean up the inevitable spill yourself.

In similar ways, our daughters begin to feel the need for independence in their preteen and teen years. There are things they want to do on their own, like choosing their own clothes, budgeting their money, planning their social activities, and getting a driver's license. While we may see where they will mess up, we must allow them space to give it a shot, even when it means picking up the mess afterward.

Seeking More Responsibility

As with independence, as your daughter develops, she may want to do things on her own and have more responsibility both at home and at school. At first, this might sound great, as we immediately start assigning her more household chores. But it also requires something big from us, a small word that is hard to execute: trust.

As our daughters take on more responsibility, they need more of our trust. Giving up that control can be scary, but it is necessary for our daughters' development. Inevitably, she will make mistakes, but she'll also learn from them. This can be as simple as allowing her to cook a family meal, babysitting her younger siblings, or giving her responsibility over an area of the house.

THE POWER OF PEER PRESSURE

Humans have a biological desire to be wanted and to belong; being alone or feeling like an outcast puts us at greater risk for harm. This need to fit in is especially prevalent in preteens and teens as they search for acceptance, figuring out who they are and where they fit in the world. These pressures, coupled with an ever-intensifying rate of social and emotional development, make our daughters more susceptible to impulsive behaviors that might go against their values or what they know to be right.

It is important to note not all peer pressure is bad. There may be times when their peers pressure them to do something positive like joining a study group or stepping out of their comfort zone to try out for a team. This is why positive influences are so important.

But what if the pressure coming from their peers isn't positive?

Equip your daughter to say no from day one. Peer pressure can start early, and their responses are rooted in how you coached them back in pre-K when they were tempted to do something they knew was wrong. If you haven't started this coaching process, start today. If resistance to peer pressure has been an ongoing conversation, trust that you've prepared them for the pressures of sex, drugs, and alcohol by having already guided them through kindergarten peer pressure. Also, remember it is an ongoing conversation. If they give in to peer pressure, it's not a failure on your part; it's a reminder the conversation needs to continue.

Become a resource to help them fight peer pressure by allowing them to use you as an excuse to get out of any situation they feel uncomfortable in. Let them know they can come to you without you judging, and remind them of the opportunity they have to share Jesus with their friends through their actions.

Physical and Sexual Development

Ahhhh, your baby is growing up! Emotional, spiritual, and social changes signal this indirectly, but physical and sexual changes are literal reminders that your daughter is no longer a little girl. During these changes, there is so much going on in her body that some days she might not even know which way is up. This is all due to that wonderful little word *hormones*. The gonadal steroid hormone estrogen and its weaker adrenal counterparts influence the physical appearance of the body as well as the brain and behavior. It's important to remember this, as there are times when your daughter may do, say, or feel things she simply cannot control.

It can be difficult to navigate what's best when your daughter doesn't know what's going on and most of the time we don't either. It is important we familiarize ourselves with some of the physical and sexual changes her body is going through so we can be there for her and hopefully explain some of what she is experiencing.

Physical Changes

Puberty and its massive physical changes can occur any time between the ages of 8 to 14, and the process can take up to four years. Everyone is different, but her physical changes will typically begin with budding breasts and growth of body hair. A girl will initially have small lumps, called buds, under one or both nipples. The breast tissue will grow and become less firm over the next year or two. Hair growth in the pubic area and armpits will also begin to occur.

These changes are concurrent with, or followed by, a noticeable growth spurt. Her arms, legs, hands, and feet will get bigger, and her body will begin to build up fat around her hips, thighs, and breasts as she develops. During this time, she may also experience an increase in oily skin and sweating. This is a normal part of physical development and can lead to breakouts of acne.

As your daughter approaches the age where these physical changes occur, it is best to begin having talks (not just one "talk") to prepare her for the coming changes in her body. You don't need to do this without assistance. There are a number of books for both you and her that can help, like *The Girls' Guide to Growing Up* by Anita Naik or *It's Great to Be a Girl! A Guide to Your Changing Body* by Dannah Gresh. You can find more online or ask for suggestions from your church.

Sexual Changes

Parents and children alike can find talking about sexual changes awkward with a capital A! What's worse, for far too long in Christian circles, the topic of sexual changes and sex in general was avoided altogether. However, avoiding conversations about sex and changes in your daughter's body only leads to an enhanced curiosity about these topics without the necessary tools to handle them. This can lead to reckless or unsafe behavior—physically, spiritually, and emotionally. Our kids will learn about sex eventually, but will we be part of their learning process, or will it be their friends, the internet, and the media?

Not only is it awkward, but many times we don't know the answers. So what sexual changes happen during puberty?

The most obvious physical change is menstruation. This begins when the body starts making hormones in preparation for reproduction. Over time, the body releases eggs from the ovaries to facilitate a pregnancy. If the egg is not fertilized, the lining of the uterus is shed, resulting in her monthly menstruation period.

In addition to physical changes during this time, they may start having more sexual thoughts and urges. We will cover this more in depth in chapter 16.

CELEBRATING YOUR DAUGHTER'S AUTHENTIC SELF

In Psalm 139:13–14, David writes, "For you created my inmost being; you knit me together in my mother's womb. I praise you because I am fearfully and wonderfully made."

The word *fearfully* when translated from Hebrew (*Yare*) means great reverence, honor, and respect, and the word *wonderfully* (*Palah*) means to be separated, set apart, unique. In other words, your daughter is strategically and uniquely created and gifted. This is not only evidenced by physical characteristics like her fingerprints, which set her apart from the 7.6 billion people on the earth and the 107 billion people that ever lived, but also in the unique way she is wired. The specific things that make her amazing make her different from everyone else.

The problem for us as parents comes when we fall into the comparison trap. We may have moments when we expect our child to be more like our friend's kid, who always makes the honor roll, or the PTA president's kid, who excels as a peer minister. When we fall into the trap of trying to make our child someone she is not, we miss the opportunity to celebrate who she is.

We live in a world that is always trying to make us into someone else, but God says He created us exactly how He wanted us. It is our job as parents to help our daughters discover how they've been created and push them to honor His gifts and celebrate their authentic selves.

Your Evolving Relationship

The good news about newborns is that their full dependence on you for being fed, changed, rocked to sleep, buckled in, and held at every cry will not last forever. The bad news is also that it will not last forever. We can get so attached to certain stages of parenting and the relationship we have with our daughters during that stage. It can be sad when your favorite stage morphs into another type of relationship. But the shift is inevitable. Our child's job is to grow up and grow apart from us.

As your relationship with your daughter becomes more hands off, it becomes more mentally and emotionally "on." At every stage, infant to toddler, pre-K to elementary, and preteen to teenager, we move a little further from simply keeping them alive and find ourselves having conversations to keep them going. Things like talking through feelings and debriefing decisions she has made might become more normal interactions. It is okay to mourn the loss of the previous stage, but we cannot allow the change to stop us from going all in at the next stage. If we fail to step into the next stage of our relationship with our daughter, we miss the opportunity to guide them through their present challenges.

Moving into a new stage can be scary, and often that comes from the fact that we've never done it before. But that is where we have the opportunity to ask God for wisdom. James 1:5 says, "If any of you lacks wisdom, you should ask God, who gives generously to all without finding fault, and it will be given to you."

As our "hands on" becomes more "hands off," we have to trust God and trust His will for our daughters even if they don't do things exactly as we'd like them to. Proverbs 3:5–6 says, "Trust in the Lord with all your heart and lean not on your own understanding; in all your ways submit to Him, and He will make your paths straight."

3

Defining Your Values and Goals

P hew, take a deep breath! I know chapter 2 was heavy, but it lays the groundwork for our next conversation: values and goals. Keep this simple rule in mind: if you don't know what you're aiming at, it is difficult to hit the target. So in this chapter, we will talk through how to define the principles that guide you and your parenting.

Raising a Woman of Christian Character

Knowing where you are going is so important. It is easy to give general advice like "stick to your values," but if you or your daughters don't know what those values are, it makes them hard to follow, especially in difficult situations where there may be a lot of social pressure. This is why it all starts with character.

The Oxford English Dictionary defines character as "the mental and moral qualities distinctive to an individual." In following this definition, Christian character would be defined as the mental or moral qualities distinctive to Christ and the mindsets and morals of His followers. When we conform our patterns of thinking and actions to those of Christ, Christian character is produced.

Some view character as irrelevant when conforming to cultural standards or going with the crowd, but character is essential to how we engage with the world, who we engage with, how we act and make decisions, and what we notice and reinforce. Without a character compass guiding us in acting out our values and morals, we can't truly be who God calls us to be.

A woman of Christian character puts others first and is motivated by love. She displays the fruit of the Spirit in her actions and attitudes. However, it is extremely important to note this does *not* mean she is perfect and does *not* mean she is just a quiet wallflower without a voice or a desire to have an impact on the world. A woman of Christian character is motivated by and values Christ, and He moves her to action.

The process of developing character begins by defining values. Kids model the values they see in their parents, which we will discuss more in part 2. For now, let's look at eight values associated with a woman of Christian character.

Love

In John 15:12, Jesus tells his disciples, "My command is this: Love each other as I have loved you." Jesus has not only commanded us to love, but He says people will know us by our love. Not by what we condemn or have policies against, but by our love—what we do rather than what we don't do. Love is at the core of Christian character. Christ loved us without judgment. He loved us freely, sacrificially, and unselfishly. It is a tall order, but it is what marks our life as Christians and should be number one when building Christian character. Loving others by serving, giving unexpected help, noticing the needs of those around us, and sharing the good news of Jesus puts feet to Jesus's command.

Patience

We live in a microwave society. If the drive-through line takes too long, the high-speed internet browser takes an extra two seconds to load a page, or we wait an extra minute in line at the grocery store because the self-checkout is closed, we get impatient.

Patience has never been easy for people, which is why it is one of the things that marks Christian character. Pausing to listen when a friend needs to be heard, waiting for God's guidance instead of forcing a dating relationship, and embracing serenity and calm instead of always having to be out on a Friday night are all part of being patient.

Kindness

In 1 Corinthians 13:4a, we get a good look at how love provides the foundation for Christian patience and kindness: "Love is patient, love is kind." Many times, the church has missed this, and for some reason, the idea of being a "jerk for Jesus" has become an actual option, as Christians have excluded or condemned others of different faiths, orientations, or lifestyles. But Jesus's ministry was marked by kindness, and He reached out to others in love. We should do the same if we claim to be followers of Jesus.

Self-Control

We've all met someone who doesn't have self-control. They can't help saying the thing they probably shouldn't say, put themselves in terrible situations, or lose their temper regularly.

Self-control shows we have more than desires driving our actions. We care more about what Jesus wants than what we want at the moment. Titus 2:11–12 says, "For the grace of God has appeared that offers salvation to all people. It teaches us to say 'No' to ungodliness and worldly passions, and to live self-controlled, upright and godly lives in this present age."

Respect

Treating others with dignity. Valuing others' worth. Giving people the reverence they deserve. Being able to respect yourself and others is a critical part of the character we should possess as Christians.

It boils down to worth and value. God is very clear that when He created humanity it was very good (Genesis 1:31). He took special time to craft each one of us before we were even born (Psalm 139:13–14). He sent His Son to die for us (Romans 5:8). You have extreme worth and value, and so does everyone else. If we truly understand that, it spills over, and we show it by how we respect ourselves and others. For girls, this could look like not giving into gossip, respecting their bodies and making positive choices about sex, or respecting their siblings' stuff and space.

Integrity

Defined as "the quality of being honest and having strong moral principles; moral uprightness," integrity is essential in living out Christian values. I like to define integrity as what you do when no one is watching. It is essentially how strong your moral compass is in pointing to true north.

Integrity encompasses many of the attributes on this list. A person of integrity is honest, respects others, keeps promises, takes responsibility seriously, helps others, is trustworthy, and more. It is also defined by consistency and the ability to do what is right even when it may be difficult or unpopular. The opportunity for integrity is found around every corner of your daughter's life: in following through on a chore she said she would do, not sneaking out after curfew, standing up for a bullied classmate, or holding true to her values when her boyfriend wants to sleep over.

Humility

Many of these characteristics are best understood when their antithesis is taken into consideration. This is certainly true when we think about a prideful person. We immediately understand why humility is so important, and the Bible confirms this in James 4:6b ("That is why Scripture says: 'God opposes the proud but shows favor to the humble.'") and Proverbs 11:2 ("When pride comes, then comes disgrace, but with humility comes wisdom.").

Our goal should be to raise women who embody humility by forgiving the girl who spread the rumor about her, looking for the best in others even when they are difficult to love, seeking peace rather than arguments when there is drama with friends, realizing their need for growth when they mess up, and leaving the judgment of the heart in God's hands.

Compassion

In Ephesians 4:32, Paul tells us, "Be kind and compassionate to one another, forgiving each other, just as in Christ God forgave you."

We have been such extreme recipients of compassion. God had tremendous concern for our suffering and sin and was willing to get involved. That is what compassion is—seeing someone's suffering or misfortune and feeling motivated to relieve it. When we understand what Christ has done for us, our response should be to have compassion for those around us.

Raising our daughters to be compassionate starts by training them to see the needs of those around them, and they will see those needs when attention to others' needs is modeled to them. When we can see the less fortunate around us and respond by serving a meal, giving a donation, or offering an encouraging word, our daughters are watching and learning how to do the same in their lives.

WHAT DO YOU VALUE THE MOST?

You are the parent. This means it's up to you to define your values. I've suggested the values that I feel define Christian character, but ultimately defining the values you will use to raise your daughter is your decision. It is a complex, serious decision that requires a lot of thought and intentionality.

To define the values you'll teach to your daughter, it's helpful to ask yourself some key questions:

- Think of a woman you admire. What values does she have that you'd like to see in your daughter?

- What values will leave your daughter most fulfilled?

- What values will please God?

- What attitudes/actions would you change about yourself? What corresponding values could you instill in your daughter so she avoids being the same way?

- Which values would you be comfortable sharing with someone you admire?

Evaluating Your Parenting Goals

Goals help us measure success and give benchmarks to shoot for. If we haven't defined our goals as parents, it's easy to lose our way.

When I was a kid, my Little League had a fundraiser with a bunch of awesome prizes for the top earner. The moment I laid eyes on the beautiful yellow-and-orange six-speed mountain bike, I immediately knew what I wanted and made it my goal to be the top earner. The prize was my motivation, but the goal was what moved me to action. I wanted to achieve and was willing to do what it took. A whole heck of a lot of phone calls and hours standing in front of the grocery store later, I rode off into the sunset on my new bike, prouder and wiser.

Moral of the story: goals create action. Many parents may know their values but may not know how they play into the goals they need to strive to accomplish. On the flip side, a goal without a value is like a hamster on a spinning wheel. You may spend a lot of time and energy, and may even accomplish the goal, but for what reason? Goals and values work hand in hand. Our values should be used as a ladder to build our goals.

Goals not only move us to action, but they also give us direction. Defining our goals as parents can be extremely helpful in knowing where we are going and evaluating how we are doing. Implementing your goals starts by clearly defining them, communicating them to the important people that will help you achieve them or stay on track with them, and repeating and revisiting them often. The chapters in part 2 will provide a little more help on achieving your goals.

Some of the most common goals people set are not necessarily biblical or helpful for their kids. Goals like making as much money as possible, placing your passions above the needs of others, and chasing perfectionism are out of sync with Christian values. Instead, here are some Christian parenting goals to consider.

Leading a Life of Faith

Walking the walk, not just talking the talk: we will discuss what this means for us as parents more in chapter 4, but one of the biggest goals we should have is living out our faith and guiding our daughters to do so as well. Parenting is not an easy task, and the best thing we can do is acknowledge that and not try to do it on our own. You'll find more success if you parent through your faith in Jesus and lean on Him to show your daughter how to do the same in her life. When you model going to church, reading your Bible, praying, or serving in a church ministry, it shows your daughter what living a life of faith looks like.

Being of Service

Jesus modeled it best: the king of the universe, who had all power and authority, came to earth as a baby. The weight of that is not lost on us as parents, as we know firsthand the helpless nature of a baby. The humility and picture of servitude conveyed in that one act show the importance of service.

If you knew you only had one day left to live, what would you do? People often give answers like eat a fancy meal, try a risky activity, or hang out with the people they love. But Jesus's life reflected the importance of service; He knew He only had one day to live, yet He chose to wash feet. It should be our goal as parents to model this to our kids and guide them toward a heart that honors servitude.

Having a Generous Heart

Actions are a manifestation of what is going on inside. Parenting goals should center around the heart, not just the actions. The act of giving is an act of generosity, which is great, but the act of continually seeking ways to serve those around you by helping with tasks around the house or church, sharing your resources, and thinking of others first instead of what just benefits you are signs of a generous heart.

Showing Christ's Love

Showing Christ's love should be a standard goal for all Christians. Jesus never said, "They will know you are my follower by how well you keep my laws," or "If you call everyone out on their sins." What He did say, however, was, "By this everyone will know that you are my disciples, if you love one another" (John 13:35).

It's a big win for parents if we model Christ's love to our daughters and they become people who model Christ's love to their world. Jesus showed His love for others by serving, loving, and blessing the poor, sick, and distressed. He gave us the ultimate example of what love looks like and what our goals should be when it comes to modeling His love. We can model Christ's love to our daughters by volunteering at a food pantry, making a casserole for someone who has lost a loved one, visiting a sick relative, or praying for a struggling friend.

Living Out a Biblical Worldview

Psalm 119:11 says, "I have hidden your word in my heart that I might not sin against you."

Many parents consider it a win if their kid turns out to be a "good person." This is a great goal, but what does it actually mean to be a good person? For Christians, a better way to say it might be "a person who sees life through a biblical lens." Our goal is to teach our daughter to use the Bible as a guide so she becomes the driver of her own moral compass instead of passing fads or peer pressure. For example, I recently spoke about a social media trend where kids record themselves damaging property, disrespecting a teacher, or exposing body parts. When these temptations surface and she is experiencing peer pressure from her friends and followers to do it, we want her to look at the situation through a biblical lens and determine it does not align with what she values.

Having Confidence in Christ

Confidence is not something that comes easily to most people. The world can be quick to tear you down rather than build you up. But our kids can have confidence in themselves as priceless, protected, beloved creations, which is to say they can have confidence in Christ. This is different from vanity, which is a confidence that thinks it's better than others. Confidence in Christ is rooted in knowing God's got your back. It's a belief in the promise of Deuteronomy 31:6b: "For the Lord your God goes with you; he will never leave you nor forsake you." It's a confidence that knows our value is derived from Christ, and not the world. If our kids can understand this and live it out, not seeking validation in the things of the world like popularity, sexual immorality, or money, then we've achieved a major parenting goal.

WHAT ARE YOUR OWN PARENTING GOALS?

Whether you adapt some of the above goals or you come up with your own, I encourage you to make sure your goals are biblically rooted, Christ following, and character producing. Also, your goals may shift as you learn and grow and certain things become more important to you. As you think through what your goals might be, here are a few questions to help you:

- How do you want your daughter to carry herself?

- What do you want your relationship with your daughter to look like?

- What do you need to do to become more like Jesus in your parenting?

PART TWO

Foundational Parenting Principles

We have talked a lot about the importance of a foundation, and we will continue to lay that foundation in part 2. This section covers foundational principles of Christian parenting and offers some practical advice that puts feet to what we discussed in part 1.

4

Modeling Your Values

*"Why do you call me, 'Lord, Lord,'
and do not do what I say?"*

—LUKE 6:46

"If you love me, keep my commands."

—JOHN 14:15

I t is no secret kids copy what they see. We have talked a lot about the impact of influences, but oftentimes we don't realize that we as parents fall into that category. Our kids will learn from us whether we actively parent or not.

The old adage "Do what I say, not what I do" simply doesn't work. Unfortunately, that is how many kids are raised. They see their parents' hypocrisy as they say one thing and do another. They see their parents set standards that they are unwilling to adhere to themselves, acting one way in public or at church and another at home. This leads to many people's decision to abandon their faith and their parents' values and run from how they were raised because they feel it was all fake.

When you truly believe something, you do it. Simple. If you own a chair that you believe is strong enough to hold your weight, you will sit in it. But if you never actually sit in the chair, do you truly believe it will hold you? It doesn't matter how much you talk about how awesome it is; the action of sitting is what proves your belief.

The same goes for what you tell your kids. If you truly believe the faith you're introducing them to, the values you preach, and the behaviors you want to see, you will live them out. Your kids know it, and they are watching to see if you truly believe what you are saying. Kids always want to test boundaries, too, and having a parent who can't follow their own rules leaves little incentive to do the same.

Being in youth ministry for the last dozen-plus years, I have seen many instances of parents sending their kids to church because it is the right thing to do, but there was no follow-through at home. They didn't practice what they wanted their kids to be—they simply put that on the church, hoping the church would instill the values on their behalf. However, 9 times out of 10, those students ended up following exactly what they were shown rather than what was taught at church. The church's single hour of influence became a moot point because of what was being modeled the rest of the time at home.

Modeling values does not mean you have to be perfect; in fact, it's quite the opposite. It means showing humility and owning when you mess up. Living out grace, mercy, and love is actually more about the honesty you show when you mess up than not messing up at all.

Modeling values is a long game. One of the biggest mistakes made when modeling our values happens when we give up or stop trying because we can't be perfect. It is a personal commitment to continually better yourself and strive to be the best you can be, and your kids get a front-row seat.

Practical Pointers

It's a heart issue. We talk a lot about focusing on the heart of our kids and not just their actions, and the same goes for us. We need to check our hearts. We need to get to the root of our actions and attitudes. If we are going to model the values we believe are important for our kids, it starts with our hearts and positioning ourselves for personal growth. Here are some ways we can work on changing our hearts:

Have a personal relationship with Jesus. Many parents want to raise kids with Christian values because they know it's good for them, but they don't believe it themselves. We are to steward our kids well by teaching them about Jesus, but the most important thing you will ever do is personally accept Jesus as your Savior. Jesus came to this earth and lived a sinless life that you and I could never live and then willingly died on a cross on our behalf to make a way for us to have a relationship with God. Jesus willingly took the punishment we deserved and offered salvation as a free gift to anyone who puts their trust in Him. If you have never done that, set this book aside right now and talk to God.

Commit to community. It takes a village! But not just to raise a kid—to keep us on track in our faith. If we are going to live out our values and model them for our kids, we need to surround ourselves with people who will point us in the right direction, call us out when we need correction, and love us through the highs and lows. Community is extremely important for personal growth, and personal growth is extremely important for living out the values we want our kids to adopt.

Give yourself grace. Jesus has given you grace; won't you give it to yourself? Oftentimes we are our harshest critics. The truth is, we will never be perfect. That's okay. When it comes to modeling values, you will inevitably have days where you fall short—you'll lose your temper, gossip about your coworker, or be overly critical of your daughter's choices. But that is where we must have grace for ourselves. Remember, it's a long game. Take a breath, it's going to be okay, you're doing better than you think. You've got this!

Be honest and humble with your kids. Not only will you mess up, but your kids will see you mess up. The mistake is not the problem; mishandling it is. Honesty and humility go hand in hand and are extremely necessary for parenting in general, but especially when it comes to modeling our values to our kids. Our kids learn how to handle failure by watching how we handle it. It is important that we are humble enough to be honest about our shortcomings. Owning our mistakes without making excuses or pretending they didn't happen—saying, "I did this and I shouldn't have, I'll do better next time"—can be one of the best lessons in teaching values to our kids.

Take a break for a heart check. Since our actions are an overflow of our heart, we need to take time for ourselves to pause and check our heart. The daily grind of parenting and life can be exhausting. This can lead to a neglect of our own spiritual health and the manifestation of that poor health in our actions. Find time to take a break, get away if you can, and check up on yourself. True, this is easier said than done when there are a million things on your to-do list. But it may be as simple as stopping at a coffee shop for 20 minutes after dropping the kids off at school, going for a walk first thing in the morning, pausing and taking some personal time before bed, or going somewhere by yourself on a Saturday morning. It is less about how much time you have and more about the intentionality of that time for your spiritual health.

What's the Word?

All throughout the Gospels (Matthew, Mark, Luke, and John) we see the role the disciples played in Jesus's story. They were there when Jesus taught, served, did miracles, fed crowds, challenged church leaders, and was arrested. The disciples lived with Jesus for three years and watched Him not just claim to be the Son of God but to live out the implications of that claim. Jesus reinforced His words with action.

As the disciples spent time with Jesus, they heard Him say things like "Love your neighbor" (Mark 12:31), "The greatest among you will be your servant" (Matthew 23:11), and "Give to the one who asks you" (Matthew 5:42). He taught beautiful lessons with His words, but then they saw Him wash their feet, have compassion, give grace, and willingly go to a cross. His actions meant even more.

Jesus had a clear moral compass that He preached about often, but that was not what made Him unique. Many people preached a moral code, but Jesus was different because He modeled it. The disciples didn't just hear Jesus's words, they had a front-row seat to His life, and that's what made Him worth following.

As parents, we are obviously not Jesus, but we can learn from His example. It was not an accident that Jesus asked the disciples to spend a large amount of time with Him. He knew they would be watching in the same way we have little eyes watching us. Words are great, but the best teacher is the one who can teach by modeling.

Actions speak louder than words, and as parents, we have an incredible opportunity to allow our actions to speak. Like it or not, our kids are watching how we live out the values we talk about and how we handle our wins and our losses.

It begins by checking our heart. Our actions are an overflow of what's in our heart, and at the core of that is our relationship with Jesus.

BIBLICAL AFFIRMATIONS

"In the same way, let your light shine before others, that they may see your good deeds and glorify your Father in heaven."
–Matthew 5:16

Follow my example, as I follow the example of Christ.
–1 Corinthians 11:1

FOR REFLECTION

1. How is your relationship with Jesus?

2. What are some ways you can intentionally surround yourself with community that will push you to be the best you can be?

3. Is there something about your parenting fails that keeps you up at night or that you're still holding on to? What would it look like for you to have grace and forgiveness for yourself as a parent?

4. What are some failures you need to own in order to have honesty and humility?

5. Pull out your calendar. Is there a time where you can give yourself an hour or two, or a couple of days, to get away and check up on yourself?

5

Establishing Trust

But I trust in your unfailing love;
my heart rejoices in your salvation.

—PSALM 13:5

Trust is one of the most important pieces to any relationship. The benefits of trust are immense, and the consequences of lack of trust are catastrophic. Without trust, we are unable to be our true selves. When it comes to parenting, when we establish trust with our kids, we free up our relationship to function the way it was meant to be.

Trust creates security and belonging. When someone trusts, there is a psychological safety that allows one to be honest and vulnerable. A girl who trusts her parents isn't afraid that something she does or says will make her parents stop loving her or not desire a relationship with her. She knows she belongs and is loved because there is a bond of trust with her parents even when they are disappointed in her actions. This is especially important when parenting girls. The security created by trust allows your daughter to let down her walls and truly experience the love she needs.

Communication is key to establishing trust. You must make it clear that what is said in confidence will not be disregarded, disrespected, or used as retaliation. Openness and honesty flourish when trust is present; it allows you and your daughter to talk to each other free of fear and judgment.

Trust isn't about lack of consequences or excessive permissiveness. Even when correction must occur, if trust has been established, your daughter knows it is from a place of love. She knows that you have her best interests at heart, even if you both disagree about what those are (and you will). When there is a lack of trust, it is emotionally exhausting. It can cause tension as you anticipate hurtful remarks or discover deceitful behavior time and again.

When I think of trust, I think of my wife and her dad. To this day, my wife has an incredible relationship with him. They take time almost every day to connect over the phone, share what is going on in their lives, and talk through any difficult situations she is navigating. I asked her the reason for their deep trust and how her dad established that trust. Her response was simple: Consistency. He always shows up, listens to her, and loves her. She trusts her dad because he keeps things steady.

As we discussed in chapter 4, one of the biggest mistakes parents make when establishing trust is that they don't model it. They say one thing and live another. When we're raising children, it's so important to be dependable and follow through on what we say.

As parents, we must realize trust is earned, not given. Maybe you have had a boss or coach who led from their position rather than their character. Being under this type of leadership is uncomfortable and demoralizing, and it feels the same way to our children. We can't expect trust to simply happen because we are the parent; it must come from our character.

Practical Pointers

First and foremost, showing our daughters we are trustworthy comes from acknowledging and showing our trust is not in ourselves but rather in God. Because humans are imperfect, we will inevitably fail, and when our full trust is in ourselves, we don't have anything to fall back on. To establish trust, we first must trust God. As Psalm 56:3–4a says, "When I am afraid, I put my trust in you. In God, whose word I praise."

There are many ways to establish trust—and many ways to break it. As parents, we often get caught up in reacting to situations rather than being intentional. But there are a few things you can do, and some you can avoid, to establish trust with your daughter:

Do listen. Listening is different from hearing; it requires action. We *hear* our kids all the time, to the point where we are sick of hearing them, but how often do we stop and listen to them? Listening means actively trying to understand your daughter and caring about the feelings involved in what she is saying. Listening helps you establish yourself as a trustworthy person in your daughter's life.

Do respond. In order to grow trust and encourage honesty, respond to her requests for help in tangible ways, like talking through the issues she's having with her friends, buying her new clothes she will feel more comfortable in, or reaching out to her teacher to inform them of bullying. You can also validate and support her feelings by listening, allowing her to express her emotions, sympathizing with what she is going through, and sharing times you have felt the same. Show her you are in her corner.

Do tell the truth. Most of us have been lied to, and we know it is the number one killer of trust. Get in the habit of not telling your children white lies such as, "There's no more candy in the house," or "Sorry, we can't watch Mickey Mouse because the TV is broken." Not only does this establish trust, but it models morals and values. Sometimes it is easier to shield our daughters from the whole truth, but practicing transparency will establish greater trust in the long term, as long as the details are age appropriate ("That's all the food we've budgeted for this month, so we have to make it last," versus "I don't even know how we are going to pay the bills.")

Do help them problem-solve. If our daughters know they can come to us with a problem and we will be their advocate in equipping them to solve that problem, they will continue to seek out our support. This is different than solving the problem *for* them, which breeds dependency and undermines confidence in their own abilities. Enabling this independence will help your daughter learn that you are trustworthy in difficult times.

Don't be quick to judge. If the only thing our daughters hear from us is how they have messed up or are doing something wrong, they will be far less likely to tell us anything. Take a deep breath, listen, and see through the lens of love before you react. A poor response will damage the trust she placed in you by opening up about her problems.

Don't blow them off. We may often feel that our daughters' problems are nowhere near the level of our own, and it can be easy to dismiss their concerns. But building trust happens when we understand that what is important to our daughters is important to us. The way they feel about things is very real and often very intense, so dismissing this or telling them their feelings are wrong only communicates that you don't understand them and they can't turn to you for help.

Don't break promises. Every time we break a promise that may not seem like a big deal to us, it gets filed away in our daughter's brain under the "I can't trust what my parents say" folder. The easiest way to avoid breaking promises is to avoid making promises you can't keep. Think twice about what you promise if you want to establish trust.

Don't flip-flop in your parenting. Remaining constant in our boundaries, morals, and values can be critical in establishing trust. Consistent structure and follow-through communicate to our daughter that we are good on our word and what we say matters. Our daughter will begin to form an understanding that we can be trusted because we are consistent.

What's the Word?

No biblical account illustrates trust more than the account of Abraham and Isaac. In Genesis 22, we see God test Abraham's faith. God tells Abraham to take Isaac, along with some wood, to the top of a mountain and build an altar because He wants Abraham to sacrifice his son. When they get to the top of the mountain, Isaac notices there is no animal for a sacrifice. Although Abraham does not want to, he puts his son on the altar, but before he can sacrifice him, an angel of the Lord stops Abraham and tells him not to go through with it. God then rewards Abraham for his faith and makes him the father of many nations.

It is a morbid story, but it shows the immense amount of trust Abraham had in God. How is this level of trust established? Through faithfulness.

God was faithful to Abraham, so Abraham trusted God. Abraham was faithful to Isaac, so Isaac trusted Abraham. *The Oxford English Dictionary* definition of *faithful* is "remaining loyal and steadfast." As we establish trust with our daughters, it is essential we remain loyal and steadfast in their lives. They need to know they can count on us.

It is a process. Stay faithful to the process so your daughter sees your faithfulness to her.

Trust is essential, and as parents, we play a very active role in establishing trust with our daughters. In wanting our daughters to trust us, we must first step out and learn to trust God. All the shortcomings that prevent our daughters from trusting us are not present with God. God is perfect, and He is worthy of our trust. Not trusting God has nothing to do with Him and every-thing to do with us. If we learn to step out and trust God, we can increase our own trustworthiness.

BIBLICAL AFFIRMATIONS

"But blessed is the one who trusts in the Lord,
whose confidence is in him."
–Jeremiah 17:7

Those who know your name trust in you, for you, Lord,
have never forsaken those who seek you.
–Psalm 9:10

FOR REFLECTION

1. What prevents you from trusting God?

2. What are some of the barriers preventing you from truly listening to your daughter?

3. From the "don't" list (page 59), what is the action you struggle with doing the most? How can you break that habit?

4. What are some steps you can take to be more faithful/ consistent to build trust with your daughter?

6

Instilling Faithfulness

Let love and faithfulness never leave you;
bind them around your neck,
write them on the tablet of your heart.

—PROVERBS 3:3

Faithfulness is the concept of consistently remaining loyal to someone or something and putting that loyalty into steady practice regardless of the circumstances. There are many things we can be faithful to: our spouse, our friends, our deodorant brand, or our favorite sports team. But our first call as followers of Christ is to be faithful to God. God desires our devotion, loyalty, and commitment to Him and wants us to instill that same faithfulness in our daughters.

God has entrusted us with the raising of our daughters, and one of the major aspects of that duty is to teach them to love and follow Jesus. The National Study of Youth and Religion, conducted over a 15-year period by the University of Notre Dame, found just 1 percent of teens aged 15 to 17 whose parents attached little importance to religion were religious in their mid-to-late 20s. Conversely, 82 percent of children raised by parents who placed great importance on faith grew up to be religiously active.

Throughout scripture, we see many examples of parents influencing their children to follow God. Hannah influenced Samuel (1 Samuel 1–2), Abraham influenced Isaac (Genesis 22), Mordecai influenced Esther (Esther 2), Eunice and Lois influenced Timothy (2 Timothy 1), Jochebed influenced Moses (Exodus 2), and David influenced his son Solomon (1 Kings 2). We, too, can instill faithfulness in our daughters. It's also important to note that not all these examples from scripture were biological parents; some were adopted parents and grandparents. Any caregiver in this role can make an incredible impact on a child's faith.

Church involvement, reading Christian books to them when they're little, devotionals and Bible studies, Christian music on the radio, and Bible clubs are all great tools for teaching our daughters faithfulness, but it can't stop there. Our faith must often be discussed, questioned, given practical application, and lived out.

As we discussed in chapter 4 (page 50), modeling faithfulness to God is the number one thing we can do to influence our daughters. The biggest mistake parents make in instilling faithfulness is not living it out themselves. Your kids become who you are, not who you tell them to be.

As parents, we must be bold in sharing our faith and instilling a sense of faithfulness in our daughters. As Romans 1:16 says, "For I am not ashamed of the gospel, because it is the power of God that brings salvation to everyone who believes."

Practical Pointers

Life happens, things get busy. Before we know it, our daughters are adolescents, acting out and chafing at our guidelines. As a parent of a teen, you may find yourself in a place where your daughter wants nothing to do with Christianity (or you). So how do we take the concept and put it into practice early on?

Besides *living it out yourself,* which, again, is the number one thing you can do, keep open the lines of communication with your daughter about faith in God. I had a friend whose daughter grew up in the church and was a committed Christian, but when she hit high school, all of a sudden the concepts she had learned in church every week were challenged. She started getting invited to parties, and not only did she begin to engage in behavior that conflicted with her core beliefs, but she also started questioning those beliefs. I remember watching my friend continue an open dialogue with his daughter to answer her questions and walk through her doubts.

Instilling faithfulness doesn't mean our daughters won't have questions and doubts and real-life situations that challenge their beliefs. This ongoing process means letting your daughter ask questions and have open dialogue about her faith or her doubts. The act of going to church will have much less value without open conversations and a safe place for her to wrestle with these concepts.

Here are a few topics and questions to get the conversation going with your daughter. Don't just rattle them off over breakfast; allow them to happen at any time: while running errands, making dinner, or riding in the car together. Let them be part of the constantly evolving process of her faith.

Talk about **consistency** often. Christianity is not a season; it is a lifestyle. Is your daughter living her faith consistently?

* What do you think it looks like to live out your faith at school? Home? On the field/court? With your friends?

* In what circumstance is it the hardest for you to live out your faith? Why?

* Have you ever had to stand up for your faith?

* When do you feel like you can't live out your faith?

Talk about **heart**, not just actions, so she understands doing the right things doesn't necessarily mean you're living for the right things.

* What is the difference between going through the motions with your faith and having genuine faith?

- Why is your heart so important?
- What does it look like to have a heart that follows God?

Talk about her **understanding of grace**. The feeling of being too messed up, unloved because of sin, or not good enough can be overwhelming enough for her to give up and abandon her faith. With a true understanding of grace, she can live faithfully, knowing God is enough.

- Which pieces of the grace puzzle are the hardest for you to understand and live? God's forgiveness? Forgiving yourself? Unconditional acceptance?
- Do you believe there are limits to God's grace? Why or why not?
- What amazes you the most about God's grace?
- What does God's grace mean for you?
- What are some practical ways to let others know about God's grace?

Talk about **authenticity**, but instead of asking your daughter these questions, ask them of yourself. Your daughter will notice.

- Am I being real?
- Am I modeling what I say in the way I live?
- What mistakes do I need to own and not pretend like they didn't happen?
- Where have I allowed religiosity to take over my relationship with Jesus?

What's the Word?

I often think about Jesus's parents. Sure, they had a leg up because their son was Jesus; He literally couldn't do anything wrong! But they did instill faithfulness, and there are a few things we can learn from Mary and Joseph.

In Luke 2:41–52, we see Jesus's family travel to the Passover festival. Jesus is about 12 years old, and as they are headed home, they realize they have lost Him. (Side note: even when you feel like you're not doing a good job as a parent, remind yourself that you've never lost the Savior of the world before.) After three days, Mary and Joseph finally find him "in the temple courts, sitting among the teachers, listening to them and asking them questions." Mary and Joseph are a little upset that Jesus left, but they realize he is exactly where he needs to be. The passage concludes in verse 52 by saying, "And Jesus grew in wisdom and stature, and in favor with God and man." This story is one of the only insights we have into Jesus as a child.

These events positioned Jesus for growth in wisdom, under-standing, and faithfulness. Jesus was in a place where he could learn. We must put our daughter in a place, like church, where she can learn and grow in her faith as well. Jesus asked His teachers tough questions, just as we must allow our daughter to ask tough questions. There was space created for Jesus to explore faith on his own, apart from his parents. This one is scary, but we must allow our daughters to live their faith on their own. Your goal should not be to make her faith dependent on you but rather for her to own her faith and make it hers.

Instilling faithfulness is a crucial yet massive task for us as parents. There are many practical things we can do to position our children for growth, but the most critical is how we live and the conversations we have.

BIBLICAL AFFIRMATIONS

Let us hold unswervingly to the hope we profess,
for he who promised is faithful.
–Hebrews 10:23

So, if you think you are standing firm, be careful that you don't fall! No temptation has overtaken you except what is common to mankind. And God is faithful; he will not let you be tempted beyond what you can bear. But when you are tempted, he will also provide a way out so that you can endure it.
–1 Corinthians 10:12–13

Let us then approach God's throne of grace with confidence, so that we may receive mercy and find grace to help us in our time of need.
–Hebrews 4:16

FOR REFLECTION

1. In what ways can you do a better job of modeling your faith to your daughter?

2. What are some areas you can get her more involved in and positioned to learn and grow in her faith?

3. Which topic of conversation is hardest for you to grasp? Why?

4. Which topic is the hardest for you to talk about with your daughter? How can you become more knowledgeable about/comfortable with this topic?

7

Setting and Respecting Boundaries

"I have the right to do anything," you say—but not everything is beneficial. "I have the right to do anything"—but not everything is constructive.

—1 CORINTHIANS 10:23

Boundaries define freedom. One of the things my kids love doing is playing in the front yard. We have a large grass area from the front door out to the sidewalk. It is perfect for running around, throwing a ball, or playing in the sprinklers on a hot summer day. The only problem is that beyond the sidewalk is the street, and in the street are cars—and you're a parent, so you understand the issue. There is major potential danger in the street, which is why the boundary line of the sidewalk is so important. My kids know they are not allowed off the grass under any circumstances. To aid in this boundary, we have a three-foot-high white picket fence.

The boundary and fence provide a framework for freedom to play in the front yard. The boundaries are not there to limit freedom but to make it possible. Boundaries instill a sense of security and help guide our daughters toward appropriate, safe behavior. The rules and routines we establish create a predictable framework that reduces uncertainty and anxiety for everyone.

Boundaries can apply to many areas—from mealtimes, bedtimes, homework times, chores, screen time, no yelling in the house, keeping your hands and feet to yourself, no jumping on the couch—to don't get in the car with someone we don't know, you can't date until you're 16, your curfew is 10:00 p.m., and no phones after bed. Boundaries really are everywhere, and some are more practical than others. A boundary is designed to set structure and give guidance.

Often, parents give up on boundaries because kids like to push them. It is easier to hold a boundary like a fence line when we know the severity of the danger on the other side, but what about the no-candy-before-dinner rule? There isn't an immediate and potentially deadly consequence like being hit by a car, so it is easy after being nagged and pushed a hundred times to just give in and give up on the boundary. One of the biggest mistakes parents make is not holding true to their boundaries. Kids learn quickly the power they have and how much their parents will budge.

Practical Pointers

Establishing boundaries can be difficult. They often aren't as clearly necessary as not playing in the street, but there are still many areas where our daughters require boundaries. Here are some steps for boundary setting.

STEP #1
Base boundaries on principles, not whims.

The "because I said so" logic tends to lead to frustration and resentment, which is why having an actual basis for our rules is so important. Go back to chapter 3 and remind yourself of what truly matters, and build your boundaries from those principles. Boundaries are more effective if we can explain the reasons behind them and the character traits they produce rather than basing them on a feeling we had in the moment. This will make your boundaries easier for your daughter to follow and easier for you to enforce because they come from someplace real. Our follow-through on boundaries requires our belief in the boundary, meaning it must have substance behind it.

Involve your daughter in the conversation.

When she understands the "why" behind a boundary and is part of the process of setting it, she has ownership over it and is more likely to heed its guidelines. For instance, when she understands the need for good nutrition and healthy eating, she may be able to be part of the conversation in deciding on no candy before dinner or candy only three days a week or whatever the ensuing boundary may be. Just remember you are the parent, and her involvement in the conversation doesn't mean she gets to run the conversation.

Clearly lay out expectations.

In relationships, jobs, and life, clear expectations are one of the best ways to avoid issues. Think about your last fight with your daughter. Was it because you expected something she wasn't prepared for or vice versa? It isn't always the case, but many times we neglect to clearly lay out expectations and then get mad when someone doesn't meet the expectations—even though they didn't even know we had them. When you establish a boundary, clearly communicate that boundary to your daughter.

Remind her often.

No need to nag, but gentle reminders about the expectation can be helpful. This doesn't have to happen through going over items on a list of rules, but rather through constant conversations about values, faith, life, and what it means to live in a way that pleases God.

Be consistent and follow through.

Setting a healthy boundary is great, but it doesn't do anything if it is not upheld and enforced. I remember being at a friend's house and having his dad look directly at us and say, "One of our rules is no climbing the tree in the backyard." It sounded like a clear boundary to me, but as soon as we went into the backyard, my friend went directly for the tree and motioned me to do the same. With apprehension, I started to object, "But your dad—" but my friend cut me off and said, "Don't worry, he won't do anything, he doesn't actually care if we climb the tree." Kids learn very quickly if we are trustworthy with the boundaries we set.

Taking the time to follow through can be inconvenient and sometimes exhausting, but don't let that stop you. Try not to fall into the naivety that your daughter won't mess up or cross a boundary. We all make mistakes, so don't assume she will always follow the rules. Be observant, and reinforce the boundaries if you need to. Most importantly, don't give up.

Look through the lens of love.

When our kids break rules or push boundaries, it is so easy for the rose-colored glasses we see our kids through to turn red with rage. But we need to remind ourselves boundaries are set because of love, and when boundaries are pushed or broken, we must act out of love in enforcing the boundaries. When we see through the lens of love, it leads us to have conversations with our daughters about why a boundary was crossed rather than just getting mad when they don't do what we want.

What's the Word?

In Exodus 20, the Israelite people are wandering the desert, having just escaped slavery in Egypt. Moses has led them to freedom, guiding them in the direction God wants them to go. One day, Moses goes up to Mount Sinai and comes down with the most famous list in history, the Ten Commandments—a list of clear boundaries he shares with the Israelite people: God should be their only God, they should respect His name, they shouldn't kill people, they shouldn't steal, they shouldn't sleep with someone else's spouse, and so on.

Why are these boundaries set? Is it to ruin all the fun? No. It is to keep the Israelites safe, give them security, and allow them to experience freedom inside the boundaries set for them. But do you notice these commandments were not just arbitrarily chosen by Moses? Yes, he was their leader, but the commandments were given to him by God.

It is our job as parents to lead our daughters, but our leadership should come from somewhere higher. When we continue to deepen our relationship with God and seek His guidance, it helps us establish the right boundaries to guide our daughters to safety, security, and freedom.

Boundaries are necessary for safety, security, growth, and a clear freedom. But setting and enforcing them can be difficult. It requires truly thinking through the *why* behind the boundaries, setting clear expectations, and following through on the consequences. It also requires lots of love, and as your daughter grows, new boundaries must be set and old ones must be evaluated to keep her safe and secure.

BIBLICAL AFFIRMATIONS

Start children off on the way they should go, and even when they are old they will not turn from it.
–Proverbs 22:6

Guide me in your truth and teach me, for you are God my Savior, and my hope is in you all day long.
–Psalm 25:5

FOR REFLECTION

1. What is the most difficult part of creating boundaries for you?

2. Can you think of any boundaries in your house that are based on whim and not principle? What can you do to change those boundaries?

3. Have you clearly laid expectations and reinforced the communication of the boundaries you expect your daughter to adhere to? How can you do a better job communicating your boundaries?

4. What would it look like for you to see your daughter's boundary crossing through a lens of love?

8

Exercising Authority and Discipline

*For this command is a lamp, this teaching is a light,
and correction and instruction are the way to life.*

—PROVERBS 6:23

Authority, discipline, respect. There is a unique relationship between these three words that produces a necessary balance when it comes to successful parenting. Authority is the power based on position to give orders, control, or rule. It sounds harsh, but in parenting, it means the power to give instruction to our children. Basically, because of our position as parent (title) we have the authority to parent (verb) our children.

Discipline is the enforcement of our parental rights of authority. It is the tool by which we teach our children to obey the rules we have set in place. Discipline is us exercising the authority we have been given to guide our children.

Respect, on the other hand, is not a given based on title. Respect is earned based on how our authority and discipline are executed. It is also reciprocated based on the level of respect that is shown. Our goal as parents should be to respect our kids and earn their respect for us, and we should view our authority and the ways we implement discipline as part of this cycle of respect.

Respect is the difference between viewing authority as a responsibility and seeing it as a right. Parents who believe they have a right to be obeyed tend to act in an *authoritarian* manner, whereas parents who view their authority as a responsibility tend to parent in an *authoritative* manner (page 8).

Authoritative parents tend to be warm, nurturing, and responsive. They have high standards for their children, set limits, and are consistent in enforcing boundaries but do it in a way that acknowledges and responds to their child's emotional needs.

Authoritarian parents are colder and less nurturing. They, too, have very high standards but believe achieving those standards comes through rules, "because I said so" logic, one-way (top-down) communication, and control.

For Christ's followers, our example of authority and discipline should be Jesus. Jesus, the King of the world, had all authority by position, but He exercised His authority through serving. Although He was never a parent, His model of loving, serving, and caring should be the basis by which we approach our authority and discipline as parents.

Practical Pointers

Life happens, emotions take over, things get hard, and the practical application of our authority and discipline can get quite messy. Try the following steps to put all this into practice.

STEP #1
Start with the relationship.

We see the best in our daughters and want to help them be their best selves. Discipline is correction for the betterment of the child, not just the enforcement of a rule. It's the difference between a coach and a very stern, authoritarian professor. Say, hypothetically, your daughter has a lapse in judgment and decides to cheat on a test, and she's caught by the professor. That professor sees their job as enforcing the rules and keeping order for its own sake. Your daughter might resent the professor's rigidness and not care very much if she follows those rules. Now imagine instead that your daughter is caught by a coach she trusts, who knows her well and has a good relationship with her. That coach might enforce consequences for the sake of what is best for your daughter and her future. If there isn't relational equity rooted in love, the discipline will only be effective in changing the behavior, not the heart. Your daughter will get better at avoiding getting caught, not at being a better person. Our discipline as parents should use a healthy relationship as its foundation. Think about a time in your childhood when you really disappointed your parents. Why did it hurt? Because you had a relationship with them and cared about their feelings, too.

STEP #2
Understand the goal.

Sometimes we forget the purpose of discipline is to produce a disciplined person. The goal of effective discipline is to foster acceptable and appropriate behavior and to raise emotionally mature adults. Keeping this purpose in mind helps us discipline properly toward a desired result rather than just for the sake of keeping everyone in line.

STEP #3
Make sure it's age appropriate.

The purpose of effective discipline is to help children develop, be able to follow rules, and acquire appropriate behavior patterns. There is no one-size-fits-all approach. Discipline must be geared toward the age, stage, and development of the child. Remember, effective discipline does not instill shame, negativity, guilt, a sense of abandonment, or a loss of trust. If the discipline is done well, it should result in a greater trust between the child and parent.

Teach self-discipline.

Again, the purpose of disciplining is not to change what your daughter has done wrong but rather instill a pattern that results in a better person who will make a better decision next time. Our discipline should help guide her to a place where she is able to be self-disciplined and help right her own ship. If we explain the reasons behind our rules and show our daughters how they might have handled the situation, they will begin to learn the tools for self-discipline.

Hold firm and follow through.

When disciplining me, my parents used to say, "It hurts me more than it hurts you." I always thought that was a load of junk. I didn't know the truth in it until seeing the look in my daughter's eyes as I had to take her toy away or seeing her tears as she sat in time-out. Disciplining hurts, but that's because we love our daughters. However, that same love requires that we push through and not give in so that our daughters are able to grow into the best versions of themselves.

Be consistent.

Consistency is one of the major keys to addressing behavior. Constantly enforcing rules can be exhausting, and it's tempting to let things slide, but stick with it. This could mean you'll need to have that difficult conversation instead of binge-watching a show, following through with taking your daughter's phone away (even though it means more work for you), or simply being aware of the rules you said you would enforce and enforcing them.

What's the Word?

Whoever spares the rod hates their children, but the one who loves their children is careful to discipline them.
—Proverbs 13:24

This is probably the most famous verse when it comes to disciplining children. However, it tends to leave a poor taste in our mouths because the words *rod* and *discipline* imply physically hitting our kids. It's understandable we think that, but it is only because we don't understand the context.

By *rod*, King Solomon is referring to a shepherd's crook, the long, sturdy stick with a hook at the end used by shepherds to catch and guide sheep. It is sometimes used to facilitate the recovery of fallen animals. It is not an instrument for hitting the animals but rather gently guiding them in the right direction.

We see reference to this device again in another famous passage, Psalm 23. Solomon's father, David, writes in verse 4, "Even though I walk through the darkest valley, I will fear no evil, for . . . your rod and your staff, they comfort me." The rod here is referred to as a comforting device. We don't often think of discipline as comforting, but being guided on the right path provides security and reassurance.

The Bible is clear on the importance of discipline, but we also see the benefits it produces in our own lives. Part of the way we as parents show our love is by stepping up and disciplining our daughters as we seek to help them become the best they can be.

As parents, we have been placed in a position of authority over our daughters, but how we exercise that authority is up to us. If we carry it out with respect, we will earn respect, otherwise we risk the opposite. Disciplining is not the fun part of being a parent, but it is critical for growth. We have the responsibility to guide, correct, and discipline our daughters toward growing into who God has created them to be.

BIBLICAL AFFIRMATIONS

No discipline seems pleasant at the time, but painful. Later on, however, it produces a harvest of righteousness and peace for those who have been trained by it.
—Hebrews 12:11

Whoever heeds discipline shows the way to life, but whoever ignores correction leads others astray.
—Proverbs 10:17

Whoever loves discipline loves knowledge, but whoever hates correction is stupid.
—Proverbs 12:1

FOR REFLECTION

1. What is the hardest part of disciplining for you? What are some steps you can take to change that?

2. Can you think of some battles you may need to step back from or concede on?

3. In what ways is your discipline pointing toward self-discipline for your daughter?

PART THREE

Targeted Parenting Strategies

In this section, we will take an even deeper dive into practical parenting. We will look at some of the common issues associated with raising girls, like self-esteem and managing conflicts, and share some strategies and advice that will help you help *her* be the best she can be.

9

Affirming Her Sense of Identity and Self-Worth

G etting everyone ready and out of the house each morning is always a struggle. One particular morning, my then-first-grade daughter was taking an especially long time getting dressed. As I headed to her room to find out what was going on, I was met by the sound of her crying. She was sitting in the middle of the floor with a pile of clothes around her and immediately exclaimed, "I have nothing to wear." I chuckled but was cut off quickly as she continued to tell me how she didn't have any fashion sense and all of her clothes weren't cute because a little girl at school told her she dressed ugly. I couldn't believe my ears because she had always been a little fashionista. But she had taken the label of "no fashion sense" and believed it as true. She ashamedly wore that label, which couldn't have been further from the truth, for years.

Labels on objects can be very useful tools: they can organize, categorize, and assign parameters to things. Labels help us know what things are, where things go, and how to use them.

Our tendency to categorize is why people are also given labels. We are told who we are, what category we fit into, and what parameters we have. Our labels are given to us by other people, by ourselves, and by society. Our daughters are also given labels that define and tell them who they are.

Labels come in all shapes and sizes: unathletic, klutz, fat, ugly, goody two-shoes, dumb, boring, weird, mean, smart, athletic, pretty. Labels impact lives. They impact the way your daughter sees herself and carries herself and how she acts in light of what she thinks about herself. But we're more than just our labels, and your daughter deserves better from the people around her. Whether it is a teacher, coach, friend, classmate, social media account, society, or even herself, no one has the right to label her.

So who has the right? The first is God, her creator. The second is Jesus, who paid the price for her by hanging on a cross. They have already given her labels, and they read, "VERY GOOD," "AMAZING," and "WORTH IT."

It is our job as parents to help our daughters believe what God has said about them over what the world says. Discovering what God says about them is the first step in taking off the false labels they have been given. When they begin to believe the truth about themselves, those false labels are debunked and begin to fall off. We need to help our daughters identify what God says and let go of what others have said that contradicts His truth.

Practical Pointers

This truth is one she needs to know but is often hard to see because of the constant pressures she faces from the world at large. As her parent, you must do all you can to help her understand her worth, value, and identity. Here are a few tips for affirming your daughter's sense of identity and self-worth.

Teach her what God says about her. If she doesn't understand her identity is not in what she has been told or what she does but rather who she is, she is fighting a losing battle. If she doesn't know where her identity comes from, she will always be searching for it. Her truth is grounded in Christ. As parents, we must teach her the gospel and what God says about her as well as remind her of these truths often. This can be as simple as making it part of your everyday conversation, reminding her before bed or before she leaves for school, making a list of Bible verses that affirm her identity and displaying it on her mirror, or listening to music that reinforces the truth of her worth.

Help her see her identity, not her actions. A few years ago, I attended a Christian recovery group with a friend who was awarded his six-month chip. As the group began, I observed something they did that was extremely powerful. Just like in AA, they introduced themselves before sharing. As they went around the circle, the person speaking would say, "Hello, my name is _____ and I am a grateful believer in Jesus Christ, and I struggle with _____." They acknowledged their issue, but they did not use it as a label to describe themselves. Their issue is not who they are. They are a grateful believer in Jesus Christ.

Your daughter will have struggles and labels, but those things don't define her, and her actions are not what Jesus sees when He looks at her. We must help her look past her label to see who she truly is—a child of God. You can help remind her of this by focusing more on her identity as a child of God than external actions and by using straightforward language such as "That is what you did, but that is not who you are."

Remind her how you view her. Our daughters' identities need to be in Christ, and His opinion of them is all that truly matters in light of eternity. However, our opinion of them carries a ton of weight, too. Tell your daughter when you are proud of her. Express to her how much you love her. Let her know the things you like about her. Positive reinforcement is amazing to hear. We love hearing it, and our daughters love hearing it as well. Don't withhold an opportunity to reinforce her identity, worth, and value.

Help her avoid the comparison trap. It is so easy to try to be someone else, but God created your daughter to be herself. Our world is clamoring for us to be someone else, but God didn't see it that way, and neither should she. When she compares herself to others, she is taking her eyes off the goal of running her own race to be the best she can be. Instead, she is focusing on what she can't be: anyone else. We can help her focus forward instead of looking laterally by reminding her of the beauty in her unique- ness, celebrating her differences, talking her through what she can control, and helping her take steps to be the best version of herself rather than trying to be someone else. Saying something like, "It's so special how you try to help your friends when they're struggling," or "I'm so proud of how hard you studied for that math test," can go a long way.

FOR REFLECTION

1. Have you given your daughter any labels that go against the ones God has given her? What can you do to reinforce God's labels?

2. What are some practical steps you can take to teach your daughter what God says about her?

3. Think of five ways you can be intentional about reminding your daughter how you view her.

4. What are some good ways to redirect her thinking when she starts to compare herself to someone else?

5. What type of work on your own identity might you need to do in order to best help your daughter with her identity?

10

Cultivating Her Passions and Interests

My wife was in second grade when her parents decided their kids would not be couch potatoes. They announced that she and her sister would be choosing a sport or activity to get them moving and out of the house. Without having any understanding of the sport or prior knowledge of how it worked, she decisively chose to play soccer. As they were a basketball family, this choice came as quite a shock to her dad, who knew roughly as much as his seven-year-old daughter did about soccer.

However, as his daughter's interest in the sport grew, so did his research. He began to frequent the library's soccer section, learning everything he could to pass along to his daughter. Not only did his daughter enjoy soccer, she excelled at it. They read soccer books, watched games, practiced in the backyard, and drove for hours to watch pro games and take notes. In her freshman year of high school, the school didn't have a coach for their girls' soccer team. Guess who stepped up? Her dad coached all four years of her high school soccer career.

We don't always share our daughters' interests, but our attention as parents can help them cultivate their passions. Philippians 2:4 says, "Not looking to your own interests but each of you to the interests of the others." Our job is to help our daughters discover what God has created them for, even if it isn't something we understand.

Practical Pointers

As parents, we walk a thin line when it comes to supporting her and pushing her away from certain interests. Obviously, there are a ton of other factors involved, but your involvement in your daughter's passions and interests do play a big role in where they go. Here are a few practical dos and don'ts for being the kind of supportive parent God wants you to be.

Head down the trail in front of you

We have tried art, gymnastics, soccer, basketball, and music, and I am sure there will be many more activities we will try with our daughters. As parents, we know our daughters' interests change, and that's okay, but when your child is interested in something, head down that trail until she's not interested anymore. The only way her interests and passions will be cultivated is if you allow her to explore them enough to figure out what they are.

This can be somewhat of a disconcerting process when your daughter decides she is not passionate anymore. Is she losing interest because her passions have changed? Because she thinks she has failed? Because her activity isn't "cool" in the eyes of others? When is resiliency required, and when is it time to head down another path? Ask your daughter direct questions about why she isn't passionate about the activity anymore. Be a critical observer of anything that may have happened to dampen her passion outside of loss of interest, and be open to the option that she really is just over it.

Impose your passion

It is so tempting to relive the glory days through your daughter, but don't. If she is into what you are passionate about, that's great! If she's not, that's great, too! In all of parenting, but especially when it comes to cultivating her interests, it is critically important to remember *she is not you*. Allow her to explore her own passions, not just follow the ones you want for her.

DO!
Provide opportunities

I had neighbors whose daughters all loved softball. They had their walls covered in posters, watched as many games as they could, and were constantly in the backyard playing and practicing. It was clear to everyone it was their passion. However, their parents never put them in a league or searched out opportunities for them to actually play. The girls were frustrated by this but respected their parents and lived out their passion in the backyard by themselves. Their parents didn't want to take the time and effort out of the family schedule for the girls to pursue that activity.

Whatever her passion or interest is, facilitate her putting it into practice. Find as many opportunities as you can (time and budget permitting!). Remember, your goal is to help her practice her passions, not to simply get a return on your investment.

DON'T!
Push too hard

We've all seen "those" parents criticizing from the sidelines. Maybe you had those parents, or maybe you already know you are that parent. But there is a difference between pushing and punishment. It is healthy to push her to be the best she can be and want her to succeed at what she is doing. However, when your desire for her to succeed becomes greater than hers, it's no longer about her. These are the types of situations where putting in the work to truly know your daughter will pay off. You want her to focus on what makes her happy, not what pleases others.

Praise her efforts

Cheer her on! Nothing cultivates a passion or interest like being acknowledged for hard work. Let her know you are proud of her. But this doesn't necessarily mean success. Help your daughter define the win, and then praise her efforts in tracking down that win.

For example, when one of my daughters first became interested in art, she had no clue what she was doing. She loved painting, but she struggled to make each project look like the teacher's example. I remember sitting on the couch next to her and asking if she was "making awesome art." She was immediately upset and a little ashamed because she didn't know how to make "awesome art," and I was already expecting it out of her. I explained that awesome art doesn't mean just making a picture that looks perfect, and while I did expect her to do her best, that's where we needed to define the "win" as her doing her best, learning more about art, and having fun. If those things were accomplished, it was a win, regardless of the outcome.

Help your daughter define what the win is for her, and praise her for her effort to achieve the win.

Judge her choices

Along with not imposing your passion on her, don't look down on her passion or interest. Even if it seems silly, unproductive, or downright wasteful to you, it's important to her, and that's what matters.

FOR REFLECTION

1. What are some of the passions/interests your daughter has that are easy to spot? What are some of her passions/interests that are a little more difficult to point out?

2. What are some of the "dos" that you have done well and should continue doing?

3. What are some of the "don'ts" that you are guilty of and need to change?

4. In general, what are some action steps you can take to help your daughter cultivate her passions and interests?

11

Equipping Her with Emotional Coping Skills

We have a wide array of personalities, emotions, and feelings in our household. All my daughters have emotional moments, but one of my daughters is just wired for empathy. From when she was a toddler, she felt things deeply, would be affected for weeks when big changes happened, and could get in a funk of emotions without even being able to explain what she was feeling or why.

She needed help understanding her emotions and how to act in light of what she was feeling. When she was pre-K and early elementary age, we had an emotion book with pictures and colors for her to flip through when big feelings hit. When she was experiencing a deep emotion, she would open the book and take a few minutes to think about how she felt, what caused it, and what she could do next. The book was a great tool to help her identify and begin to understand her emotions, and it was a great conversation starter for my wife and me to help process what she was feeling.

Processing emotions is not an easy task for anyone, but for a kid or adolescent who may be experiencing an emotion for the first time, it's easy to get overwhelmed. As parents, we try to help them process, but ultimately we want to equip them to do it themselves. Coping is not something we are born knowing how to do. It is a skill we learn with practice, and it is never too late to start teaching your kids healthy coping strategies that will aid in dealing with life's ups and downs.

My dad was very intentional about teaching me the skills needed to fix a car. I can change a tire, change the oil, and name many of the parts under the hood. Am I an expert mechanic? No. Can I handle an emergency? Yes. The same goes for teaching your daughter the skills needed to process her emotions. You need to help her process these emotions now but also prepare her with the skills needed to manage them throughout life.

Practical Pointers

Helping your daughter identify, express, and cope with her feelings is a process. However, it can be a touchy process because emotions can be volatile and cloud our judgment, making us say and do things we might otherwise not. As parents, we must be willing to wade into difficult conversations and help our daughters develop coping skills even if it's messy.

These conversations are a critical part of the process, but how do we have these conversations? When your daughter is overwhelmed, either with details or intense emotions, help her break the problem down. Being able to step back and look at the situation and identify stressors and emotional responses is an extremely valuable tool. Here are some conversation starters to help your daughter reflect on what she's feeling and what she wants to do next:

- Describe the situation to me from a third-party point of view.

- What about the situation stresses you out? What makes you mad? Is there anything good in this situation?

- What does God say about the problem?

Then turn the conversation into an opportunity to label the feelings she is having. It can be hard for her to fully acknowledge or understand what she is feeling, especially when she is younger. However, pausing and labeling those feelings can be extremely helpful for her.

- What is the main emotion you are feeling right now?

- What else is going on? What else are you feeling? Is that part of it?

- How is the main emotion you are feeling influencing your thoughts right now?

Helping her understand that emotions are valid but that they can also distort her thinking is an important part of coping with them.

- Do you think your emotions match what's going on?

- How do you think someone else in your situation should act?

- I'm not saying you can't feel that way, but what do you think is a better way to show it?

Positive practices such as self-talk and breathing exercises can also play a huge role in coping with emotions and overwhelming situations. Some are questions, some are guided activities, but here are some prompts to help her learn these practices.

- Let's think of some positives in this situation that are different from what you are feeling. Speak that truth over yourself and the situation.

- Take a deep breath and hold it for five seconds, then exhale and try to say one positive thing. Do this five times.

- Try to clear your thoughts to focus on the breathing.

1. What are some areas in your life where it has been difficult to control your emotions?

2. What are some of the techniques or coping skills you have used to best control your emotions?

3. What does your daughter struggle with most from this chapter? Understanding what she's feeling? Processing? Moving on?

4. Think through and maybe jot down a few places/situations where you can see yourself sitting down and having these conversations with your daughter.

5. What are a few actionable steps you can take to help your daughter with emotional coping skills?

12

Maintaining Strong Family Bonds

"Get your homework done." "Get ready for practice." "Get ready for bed." If your family is anything like mine, getting through life can feel like a mechanized assembly line. But I think we would all agree that strong family bonds are the goal you would like to see in your family. The Bible doesn't have many specific scriptures on the nuclear family; however, it does have many on how we should treat people close to us:

Be completely humble and gentle; be patient, bearing with one another in love. Make every effort to keep the unity of the Spirit through the bond of peace.

—EPHESIANS 4:2–3

And over all these virtues put on love, which binds them all together in perfect unity.

—COLOSSIANS 3:14

As a pastor's family, we have done our share of moving. Moving is not fun, and each move has its own challenges as we leave behind the family, friends, and community we have made. As we were going through one of our moves, I remember apologizing to one of my daughters, who was eight years old at the time. I told her I was sorry she had to leave her school, her classmates, her friends, and the house she was used to. I will never forget her response as she looked back at me and replied, "It's okay, Dad. As long as we have our family, we will be all right."

She was right, and I was totally fist pumping as I realized how much of a win it was to have strong family bonds instilled in my daughters. I resolved I would always be willing to put in the work needed to create and strengthen those bonds.

Past the obvious advantages of having one another to lean on and spend time with, there are many benefits to strong family bonds—no matter who you live with, love, or call your family. They encourage better behavior in children, can lead to improved academic performance and strong communication, help keep families united, promote happiness, and provide a critical support system. We could spend hours listing all the obvious benefits of strong family bonds, but are we spending the time needed to create those bonds? Strong family bonds don't happen by accident—they are the result of much time, energy, and effort. How can we do it?

Practical Pointers

The time, energy, and effort needed to create strong family bonds manifest through intentionality. Here are a few ways you can be purposeful about using your time and activities to build strong family bonds:

Eat meals together. Meals are a surefire way to slip in regularly scheduled family time because everyone needs to eat. They can also be an excellent way of creating routine in the life of your family. Routine creates stability and forms bonds, which can be a major win. Plus, food makes people happy, which makes conversations a little easier (unless you have a picky toddler!). If you have teenagers busy with friends and activities, you may need to get creative. Set a time and put it on everyone's calendar, only scheduling it two or three days a week, saying no to other things to prioritize mealtimes, or shifting around mealtimes to accommodate everyone around the table.

Schedule family time. Bonds form from relationships, and relationships form by time spent together. But life gets busy, and outside of your regular routine it can be very difficult to get intentional family time. Scheduling family time helps make sure it will happen. Whether it is a week at the lake, a day hike, a movie night, a weekend drive, or even just a walk around the block, it is important to make specific time for relationship building. If you're having trouble finding time to relax together, try teaming up for everyday tasks, like trips to the grocery store or prepping dinner. Either way, do it, schedule it, make it happen, and be present together, not allowing other things like your phone to take the attention it requires.

Deal with issues. Adversity is necessary for growth. Busy families tend to prioritize keeping the peace instead of the more difficult task of resolving conflicts. Create a culture of dealing with issues by not allowing them to be swept under the rug. Have tough conversations, and love one another enough to be real with them. We will also talk more about conflict resolution in chapter 13.

Huddle up. Schedule specific time to get on the same page, check in on one another's calendars and to-do lists, and stack hands as a team. It doesn't have to be long or super planned out, but think of it as a huddle before the play in football. It's not the main thing, but it helps make sure everyone is ready for the main thing.

Encourage and support one another. Family should always celebrate one another's wins, cheer for one another's successes, and be there for one another when a little extra love and encouragement is needed. Make a habit of simple things like encouraging your kids to show up to one another's games and performances, talking about their achievements or positive moments around the dinner table, and acknowledging when someone in the family needs an extra word of encouragement or one-on-one ice cream date to talk.

Find a common mission. Bonds are formed when people are headed in the same direction and share a common goal or purpose. That is why teams, with members from all different backgrounds and walks of life, can become like family. Volunteer at a food bank, go on a mission trip together, have family goals to serve your community or reach your world for Christ. Work toward a common goal as a family so bonds can form and good can happen.

Do fun things together. Bonds are also formed when fun happens. Laughter breaks down walls. When the girls were little, I remember making a blanket fort while they were napping and watching them wake up to a magical new world in our living room. Or, as they got older, surprising them after school with movie tickets, mini golf outings, or an unexpected picnic in the park. As they got older, the fun activities changed, but the principle stayed the same. When you have fun with your family, bonds begin to form. The bonds are not built on the fun, but the fun brings them out.

FOR REFLECTION

1. What are a few ways you have seen bonds help your family?

2. Do you find it hard to get family time? Why or why not?

3. What activities mentioned in this chapter caught your attention the most? What are some actionable steps you could take in the next week?

13
Managing Conflict

I probably shouldn't have said what I said. Now the door is slamming behind her and she's storming out. I'm just sick of it; it feels like it has been weeks of dealing with the same issue that only leaves us not seeing eye to eye. I understand she is mad, too, but I'm her father. Where's the respect? I know I am right, and she just needs to see that. But maybe that's the problem. Maybe I share some of the blame, but now it's such a mess, I don't know what to do or how to turn it around. Even if I try, will she even listen or want to fix it?

I know she's mad and things aren't great between us. I bought her favorite food and stocked the freezer. Hopefully her mood changes and things just fix themselves. Ugh, that didn't work. Now I have a bunch of Bagel Bites, and I'm still going to have to yell at her again until she sees things my way. I don't want to give in and let her win—that won't teach her anything. But maybe that's the only way to move forward. I'm just not sure.

Maybe you can relate. Maybe you've had similar interactions, or maybe your interactions have been way worse. Or perhaps you haven't encountered conflict with your daughters yet, in which case, buckle up—it's coming. Conflict can be such a difficult road to navigate. It seems as if there is no path to reconciliation, but there is.

We serve a God of reconciliation. God took our conflicts with Him and gave everything to reconcile us to Himself. Because we are made new in Him, we now have a responsibility to be agents of reconciliation in our lives, especially when it comes to our family. There are strategies we as parents can use and conversations we can have to point our daughters toward reconciliation and managing the conflicts we have.

Practical Pointers

Managing conflict doesn't happen by accident. It takes us as parents stepping up and leading the way by initiating conversations that lead us to reconciliation. Here are some step-by-step instructions that might help you get to the bottom of conflict, settle it, and move forward.

STEP #1
Clarify the source of conflict.

Almost always, the source of conflict is a miscommunication or lack of clear communication around expectations. You are mad or your daughter is mad because an expectation has not been met, disappointment has occurred, and you don't see the other's perspective. Conflict cannot be fixed unless the source of the conflict is called out. Once we get to the bottom of what the actual problem is, which is not always what it appears to be, we are able to fix the issue. Get to the bottom of things by first understanding your daughter's emotional process and knowing the right time to ask the right questions. When she is ready, find the source by asking, "What made you feel this way?" "Did someone say something or do something to hurt your feelings?" "Do you feel like you're being heard?" or something along those lines.

STEP #2
LISTEN.

When we listen to the other person and hear how they view things, we can discover how the miscommunication or misunderstanding is happening. Our tendency is to want to be heard. To resolve the conflict, we must follow the adage "Be quick to listen, slow to speak." Be an active listener who doesn't simply hear words but truly seeks to understand what the other person is feeling and where they are coming from. During these conversations, I am usually constantly repeating in my head, "Listen, don't speak," and "See it from her point of view."

STEP #3
Fight fair.

This is important to remember in the middle of a disagreement. During any conflict, but even more so in a conflict with your daughter, focus on the conflict at hand and don't bring up old issues. Don't allow the disagreement to make its way into name-calling or slandering, don't interrupt, don't intentionally exploit weaknesses for your personal gain to win the argument, and don't gossip about your daughter or take your disagreements to other people.

As the parent, often you must be the one to set the standard of fighting fair. Keep the outcome in mind, and constantly ask yourself if what you are saying or doing is helping you achieve the outcome or simply making you feel better in the moment.

Be willing to die.

Okay, let me explain this one. Regardless of what you may be thinking or feeling during an argument, I am referring to the idea of dying to yourself. The concept of "dying to self" is found throughout the New Testament. It is the idea of setting down our wants and desires to pursue the greater goal of serving Christ. When it comes to conflict resolution, the greater goal is resolving the conflict, which will require one or both parties to lay down what they desire. As the parent, be willing to die to self where you can, but also work on instilling that idea in your daughter. Truly resolving conflict involves both parties understanding what it means to die to self and seeing the conflict through that lens.

STEP #5
Agree on a resolution.

"Well, we aren't fighting anymore, so I guess it's all good." Too often this is the attitude present in conflict resolution, but if you are honest, this is not a resolution. *Resolution* is defined as "a firm decision to do or not to do something," which requires a clear definition and action. To fully resolve the conflict, you must determine who will do what for the situation or problem to be taken care of. Agree on a solution, and clearly lay out what that solution is and what it means for both parties involved.

1. What is the most common source of conflict in your household?

2. What are some ways you can actively listen to your daughter during conflict?

3. What are some ways you have not fought fair in the past? How can you change that and start to fight fair in the future?

4. What would it look like for you to be "willing to die" in times of conflict in your house?

5. What are some actionable steps you can take this week to better manage the conflict in your household?

14

Boosting Her Self-Esteem and Self-Respect

M y first published book was called *Jesus-Colored Glasses: Seeing Our Worth and Value in a World That Doesn't.* Our world tells us everywhere we go that we are not enough: not smart enough, not pretty enough, not talented enough, the list goes on. Obviously, this is not an adolescent problem; it is a human problem. However, it is intensified during adolescence.

What you believe about your worth and value, or self-esteem, affects how you respect yourself. When you live with no self-respect, you tend to care less about the decisions you make, the situations you put yourself in, and how you expect to be treated. If you don't have value, then why respect yourself? Who cares what you do or allow to be done to you?

Many teenage girls lie in bed at night and have this reality hit them hard. They may buy the most fashionable clothes, tell the best tall tales, or pretend to get better grades than they do. They are often willing to do whatever it takes to look cool and fight off the feeling of worthlessness. But it doesn't always work. They may still dislike their appearance, believe they're not good enough at sports, not get the attention of their crushes, or struggle to pass tests. They may still feel like they have no value.

But when God looks at us, He sees a masterpiece.

This is shown in Psalm 139:13–14, which says, "For you created my inmost being; you knit me together in my mother's womb. I praise you because I am fearfully and wonderfully made; your works are wonderful, I know that full well." Paul also makes this point in Romans 5:8: "But God demonstrates his own love for us in this: While we were still sinners, Christ died for us."

When God looks at us, He sees someone with extreme worth and value, someone worth sending His Son to die for. As parents, we must help our daughters put on Jesus-colored glasses and see themselves the way God sees them.

Practical Pointers

Worth comes from God but is challenged by everyone. Your daughter will go into a world that will constantly tear down her self-esteem and self-respect. Your job as a parent is to help her rebuild. Here's how:

Help her discover her gifts. Everyone is good at something. Your daughter has been specially gifted with a talent, unique quality, or passion. When she can operate inside of her gifting, not only will she find fulfillment, but she will also be taking a step toward seeing herself the way Jesus sees her.

You can try to get her involved at church or in an activity that explores her talents. If she's unsure, point out to her the things you see in her that she may not have seen in herself, and support her in activities, as we talked about in chapter 10 (see page 87). Remember, everyone is different, and your approach in how you nudge, push, praise, or steer your daughter into discovering her gifts needs to be tailored to her. What does she respond to best?

Help her cultivate positive relationships. The people she surrounds herself with can either help her build self-esteem and self-respect or tear them down. Ask your daughter intentional questions about how her friends make her feel, what they say to her, and if they are a positive support of her self-esteem. Showing an interest in her friends beyond just trying to police who she hangs out with is a good start to getting her to open up about her friends.

Help her realize love is unconditional. Nobody is perfect. The good news is God's love for us is not dependent on our performance. In fact, it is in spite of our performance. Paul reminds us in Romans 3:23 that "all have sinned and fall short of the glory of God." We hear a similar message in Isaiah 64:6: "All of us have become like one who is unclean, and all our righteous acts are like filthy rags." Sounds pretty bleak, right? Well, God loves us and sees extreme value in us anyway! When your daughter is feeling down about herself, remind her of God's love. Tell her of a time you've messed up and felt His support, let her know her failures do not define her, and help her see she is loved by the way you treat her.

Help her serve others. When we serve others and think of them above ourselves, we shift our focus to them instead of only seeing ourselves. Turning our lens outward not only keeps us from fixating on our shortcomings or perceived inadequacies, but it also opens our perspective to the good we are doing and helps build our self-esteem. Help your daughter find opportunities at church, school, in the community, or by going on a mission trip. Choosing activities her friends are enrolled in can help, so consider speaking to her friends' parents for ideas as well.

FOR REFLECTION

1. What are some ways you can help your daughter see her giftings?

2. Which of your daughter's friends are a negative influence on her self-esteem? Which are positive?

3. How can you show love and support after she's made a mistake?

4. What are a few ways you can help her find opportunities to serve others?

15

Combating Negative Body Image

My daughter was five years old when she first asked what "chubby" meant and if she was chubby. I don't know where she heard it, but not loving ourselves and our bodies seems as if it goes hand in hand with being alive. Everyone has something they would change about themselves.

When I was in school, I remember feeling about an inch tall because of my acne. I felt gross and wanted to hide it as much as I could. I remember summer after summer sitting by the pool at friends' houses so I wouldn't have to take my shirt off and expose the acne on my back, the thing I hated most about myself. Everyone would swim, and I sat in a chair beside the pool watching everyone else have a blast. When anyone asked, I would just claim I didn't feel like swimming that day. But in actuality, I didn't like myself. I am sure you can think of a story like this in your own life as well.

In a culture that places so much value on physical appearance, especially for women, there is a thin line between how we view our body and how we view ourselves. But our worth is bigger than our body, and as parents, we need to help our daughters understand how to celebrate their beauty in that light. Remind your daughter of Genesis 1:27: "So God created mankind in his own image, in the image of God he created them." That is a major compliment! When the thought of her image becomes your daughter's nemesis, she needs to remember she was created in God's image. Let's help our daughters understand why this is a beautiful thing.

Practical Pointers

Your daughter will likely grapple with negative body issues no matter what. And while we always want to help, we should be aware there are things we can do that make things worse, too. Here is a list of dos and don'ts that will help guide both of you through this difficult topic.

DO!

Redefine what beauty means

If there wasn't a standard to compare to, there wouldn't be body image issues. When Adam and Eve tried hiding from God because they were ashamed and naked, God's response to them was, "Who told you you were naked?" Today, the world is telling your daughter what beauty is (and it's always a moving target) through her friends, her peers, and her media. As her parent, you need to rewrite the standard she is subscribing to. Affirm her by telling her the things you are proud of her for, and place a high value on her inner qualities by reminding her she is smart, funny, caring, or compassionate to help her navigate these mixed messages.

DO!

Remind her there's no such thing as perfect

Everyone has flaws. There is literally no such thing as a perfect body. Even the celebrities and influencers we deem "perfect" are subject to insane amounts of Photoshop, filters, makeup, and hundreds of angles to find the right picture. Talk to your daughter about the false nature of what she is seeing. Have a conversation with her about the standard of "perfect" that doesn't exist and how this makes her feel. As parents, we should also avoid idolizing the looks of celebrities or even people we know personally.

Highlight what is unique

Everybody is unique. For the most part in our society, being different is viewed as being outside the "standard" and can actually contribute to body image issues. However, your daughter's uniqueness should be celebrated. She may not look like everyone else—but that is amazing. Help her see the beauty in her uniqueness by accepting your own special qualities and modeling what you would like her to do. Be a safe place for her to live in her uniqueness by not making fun of the things that make her unique or judging her for doing things differently than you.

DON'T!

Ignore social media

One of the biggest pushers of modern beauty standards is social media. Your daughter sees what gets likes and wants to be that regardless of whether or not it is realistic. Establish healthy boundaries by setting time limits on social media using parent control settings, noticing when she is spending large amounts of time on her phone, and talking about the importance of limiting her time on social media—and why.

DON'T!

Focus on her appearance

It's wonderful to hear compliments about our appearance. Everyone wants to feel attractive, largely because our society places such a premium on it. But focusing on your daughter's appearance often, even if it's complimentary, can send her the message that a large part of her value lies in what she looks like. Your comments steer your daughter's perception of herself, so the message can be even more damaging if your speech is negative.

If you feel the need to help with her appearance, use practical, nonjudgmental statements like "We need to brush your hair right now," rather than "Your hair looks sloppy," or "That doesn't match."

Instead of mentioning her appearance, focus on positive aspects of her character, like complimenting how hard she's worked on a project or a situation where she's shown kindness.

DON'T!
Speak negatively about yourself

Avoiding negative speech about physical appearance also applies to yourself. Body image is something we all struggle with, but when you say something negative about your own body or appearance, remember your daughter is watching. As discussed earlier in this book (page 50), children model what they see their parents do. When your daughter hears you criticize yourself, she is learning to treat herself that way, too. Be kind to yourself, and think about what you say in order to help your daughter see herself in a positive light.

FOR REFLECTION

1. What are some steps you can take toward limiting outside influence on her beauty standard?

2. How do you talk about your own appearance? Is it positive or negative?

3. What comments or actions have you had about your or her appearance that you need to stop?

4. What are some action steps you can take to help your daughter combat negative body image?

16

Broaching Love, Sex, and Relationships

I grew up playing baseball. As a kid, I sought to learn as much as I could wherever I could. I attended many clinics and had personal coaches. Both the clinics and the coaches were helpful, but they were very different.

The clinics were full of great drills and tips, but they were usually a one-day, hope-it-worked, see-you-later type of event. On the other hand, a personal coach was able to walk with me. He was there for continual support as I grew, so he was able to help me at any stage and could address any issues with my swing or pitching motion as they came up.

Talking to your daughter about love, sex, and relationships should be more like a personal coach and less like a clinic. It is a continued conversation. Having "the talk" one time is good for giving information, but it doesn't really guide her in navigating the difficulties of these experiences. For far too long, and most likely in the generation you grew up in, Christians avoided the topics of love, sex, and dating. Parents knew they needed to talk about it, so they geared up for one big "talk" (by which time you probably knew everything already) instead of making it a continual topic of conversation. But a coach is better than a clinic, which is why it is our responsibility as parents to broach the topic early and often.

As you approach these conversations, don't shy away from addressing the pressure she will face from friends, society, or boys to have sex outside of God's design. Talk about God's design, and help her understand 1 Corinthians 6:19–20: "Do you not know that your bodies are temples of the Holy Spirit, who is in you, whom you have received from God? You are not your own; you were bought at a price. Therefore honor God with your bodies." Remind your daughter of the importance of a dating partner that respects her values and boundaries, and let her know she can come to you with the questions and issues she might have.

Practical Pointers

I get it, having this conversation can be awkward and embarrassing for everyone involved! But the way we break through this is by continually pursuing the conversation. The more you talk about it, the less awkward it is.

But how do you even approach the conversation? Here are a few tips and topics to cover as well as questions to get the conversation going.

Create open lines for conversation and questions

Your daughter will find the answers to her questions no matter what. You need to ask yourself if it will be you, her friends, or Google that answers them for her. Creating a place for her to safely ask questions without fear of judgment or anger is extremely important.

ASK HER . . .

1. What do you know about love? Dating? Sex?

2. What are you hearing from the people around you about love? Dating? Sex?

3. How can I help answer your questions about love? Dating? Sex?

4. Why is it weird for you to come to me about love? Dating? Sex? What can I do to make it less weird?

Define Love

I recently saw a car with two bumper stickers. One was "Jesus loves," and the other read "I love my pugs." While loving your dog is great, it can't compare to Jesus's love shown by dying on a cross for all of humanity. True, Christlike, mutually respectful love is difficult to understand when in society we say we love pizza and our new pair of jeans the same way we say we love our grandma and the boy or girl we just started dating. So what is love? We must help our daughters understand what love is, what it means, and how to navigate it.

ASK HER . . .

1. Describe to me what you think love means. How does love play out with the different people in your life?

2. What's the difference between loving pizza and loving a person?

3. Let's look at what the Bible says about love in 1 Corinthians 13. What do you think about that type of love?

Lay Out God's Plan for Sex

Sex is good, God is good, and God's design for sex is good. God's design for sex (sex inside the covenant bond of marriage) is not intended to lessen the fun and enjoyment of sex but rather enhance it and allow us to experience it to the fullest. Be willing to let these questions springboard into conversations about God's design and what it means for your daughter.

ASK HER . . .

1. What do you think God thinks about sex?

2. If sex is a good thing, why would God put guidelines around sex?

3. How do you think you can live out God's plan for sex in your life?

Think about the Why behind Dating

I was at a loss for words when one of our daughters came home from first grade and was talking about who was dating whom in her class. First grade! The terms "dating" and "going out" are thrown around but not always understood. Talk to your daughter about the purpose of dating beyond just the feelings of attraction. The truth is, dating is to help you discover if the person you're interested in is a good match for marriage, but you can also help her think about the intentionality behind setting boundaries, learning how to respect each other, and communicating well.

ASK HER . . .

1. What do you think the purpose of dating is?

2. When do you think you are ready to live out the purpose of dating?

3. What are some of the possible dangers in dating?

4. How can I help you when it comes to understanding dating?

FOR REFLECTION

1. What is the scariest part of talking to your daughter about love, dating, and/or sex?

2. Where are some good places/times you could start talking to your daughter about love, dating, and/or sex?

3. What are some areas where judgment creeps into your conversations? How can you work to create a safe place for her to talk about love, dating, and/or sex?

4. How can you best keep the conversation going with your daughter?

17

Navigating the Internet and Social Media

Most parents of little kids can relate to the panic that occurs when a relative who doesn't have kids invites you over. Not every house is suitable for little kids. In fact, I remember all the work that went into making our house baby- and toddler-proof. Sharp edges that needed covering, baby gates that needed to be installed, cabinets that needed to be locked, doors that needed to be secured, and items that needed to be moved were just a few of the looming dangers that required our attention. Our job as parents was to help our kids avoid the potential dangers around them.

We live in a digital world now, but our job as parents is the same—to help our kids identify dangers and make decisions that will keep them safe. Our daughters face cyberbullying, identity theft, catfishing, mass distribution of pornography and other offensive images/messages, and scams. There is also a strong link between social media and an increased risk for depression, anxiety, loneliness, self-harm, and even suicidal thoughts as we chase validation and likes. It's a scary list. So how do we keep our daughters safe?

Practical Pointers

It may seem overwhelming, but by being proactive, establishing boundaries, staying aware, and communicating often, you can get ahead of the dangers and help your daughter traverse the difficult terrain of today's technological world.

Parents' To-Do List:

☐ **Teach and equip your daughter**

If we're honest, our daughters probably know more about the internet and social media than we do! But this is where having open conversations with them is extremely important. Discuss what is out there in the way of new apps, sites, and social media outlets. Do your research, but also learn from her; allow your conversations to be a two-way dialogue.

When you learn what is out there, discuss the possible dangers of that platform, app, or site (cyberbullying, catfishing, trafficking, sexting, scams, inappropriate images, etc.), and help her understand the whys behind internet safety. Making rules is great, and we will get to that in a second, but equipping her to understand the possible dangers and the reasons behind the rules will help her police herself and stay out of potentially risky situations. Encourage her to set boundaries based off your discussions and be active in the safety process.

☐ **Establish tech-free zones**

Technology is awesome, but it tends to get in the way of face-to-face human interaction. As you seek to be relational with your daughter, establish times and places where phones, iPads, laptops, and other digital devices are off limits. These might include bedtime, mealtimes, a family night, a certain room where family meetings or social time happens, church, or car rides. You decide where and when the tech-free zones are. Build in space where she is able to be free from tech.

☐ Tap into parental controls

The capabilities of parental controls on devices are mind-blowing, especially for parents of younger girls just starting out with their own social media accounts. You can be involved, set boundaries, track use, limit time, and more. Explore how parental controls work, and utilize them as the amazing tool they are. Another tip is to follow her accounts. Be aware of what she is doing, posting, liking, and so on.

Your Daughter's To-Do List:

☐ Know it's real life

The internet and social media are accessed through a screen, but what is said and done has implications in real life. People tend to think that if it said through a keyboard, it doesn't hold the same amount of weight, but the truth is, it holds more because it doesn't go away. Your daughter should know that what she does on the internet has real-life consequences.

☐ Know it's fake

Did I just totally contradict myself? Not really, let me explain. While our online actions may have real-life implications, most of what we see is not an accurate representation of real life. Too often we compare ourselves to others based on fake portrayals of others' lives. Anyone can post anything; it doesn't have to be true. For example, someone could be having the worst day of their life: their dog dies, their partner breaks up with them, they fail a test, and they crash their car. But they take a picture of the sunset and post it with the caption "Life is just chasing sunsets" and everyone seeing it is jealous that their life isn't as awesome. Your daughter needs to know what she sees is not real. At best, it is a highlight reel, but most likely it's just fiction.

☐ Know her identity is in Jesus, not likes

Your daughter needs to know where her worth and value come from, and it is not the internet and social media. It is such an easy trap to fall into when she doesn't get likes or feel as cool as someone else online, but it is critical she understands love over likes and value over views. Her identity is in Jesus, not social media.

☐ Think before she posts, likes, or follows

What is put out there stays out there. Her social media account becomes her personal brand, which means it represents her. College recruiters, potential future employers, and prospective friends or boyfriends are all able to judge her and her character based on what her social media says about her. Your daughter needs to understand that and think before she posts, likes, follows, or comments on online content.

☐ Reflect her heart

Because it is real life and it does represent her, it also provides a looking glass into her heart. Matthew 12:34b says, "For the mouth speaks what the heart is full of." Translation for today's day and age: "What you do online and on social media shows what's going on in your heart." How's your daughter's heart?

FOR REFLECTION

1. Are you creating a space where she can talk about what's going on in the world of the internet and social media without fear of judgment or a lecture?

2. What areas do you need to learn more about the internet and social media so you can talk with your daughter?

3. How can you be a better listener to your daughter when it comes to the internet and social media?

4. In light of this chapter, what are some practical ways you can help your daughter live out her faith online?

18

Diving In When Your Daughter Is Acting Out

I had spent many hours sitting at fast-food restaurants watching my daughters entertain themselves on the play structures, but on this particular day at Chick-fil-A, it was different. As I finished my #3 (12-piece nuggets, waffle fries, and half lemonade, half Sprite), I noticed there was a very rowdy boy well over the size and age limit in the play area with my daughters. As I was about to say something, he pushed a kid at the top, who stumbled back and created the domino effect of one kid stumbling into the next. All the kids stayed on their feet except my two-year-old at the back of the line. One small push and she went tumbling backward down the stairs. As she crashed to the bottom, her screams came out almost simultaneously. I immediately ran to scoop her up and come to her aid. She needed me, and I had to get to her.

My precious baby was hurt. In that moment, I was acting like a first responder, running toward the problem rather than away from it. This can seem crazy to some of us who are not first responders; it's not how we are wired.

However, as parents, we are the first responders. Not just physically but emotionally and spiritually. When I heard my daughter cry, I knew she needed me. It's the same when your daughter is acting out; she is essentially crying that she needs you. It is much easier to run the other way, and sometimes everything in us is screaming to do just that. But when your daughter begins to act out, it is your job to dive in.

As I was doing research for this book, I came across a Christian parenting book from the first decade of the twenty-first century. The back cover of the book basically said that parenting is not complicated or hard, and if it is difficult, you're doing something wrong. For too long, this has been one prevailing attitude from Christians when it comes to parenting, and it could not be further from the truth.

Parenting will be hard. Your daughter will talk back, argue disrespectfully, have outbursts, break curfew, and act unsafely. You will want to give up, give in, and not come to her aid when stuff hits the fan. But when it gets difficult and your daughter starts acting out, she is actually crying for your help. She is telling you through her actions and attitude that something inside is not right and she needs her first responder to dive in and help with the situation.

God has given you the gift of your daughter, and He has entrusted you with the responsibility of raising her even when it is hard. Dealing with out-of-control behavior is brutal, but God placed you exactly where you are for a reason, and He needs you to rise to the occasion and dive in even when it's difficult.

Practical Pointers

Where do you even start? When she is acting out, the entire atmosphere of the house can feel like World War III, and finding a bomb shelter to protect yourself seems like the best option. But there are a few steps you can take to calm and resolve the situation. Here are some steps for diving in.

STEP #1
Give yourself grace.

When your daughter acts out, it is so easy to ask yourself what you did wrong. We put the blame for her behavior on ourselves, which can make us feel inadequate as a parent. However, you need to give yourself grace—not only in the fact that she is acting out, but also in how you handle it. Diving in can be messy, so go easy on yourself and view your daughter with grace as well.

STEP #2
Stay calm.

Trust me, I understand how easy it is to overreact when your daughter is acting out, especially in her teenage years. Teens can be difficult, annoying (if we're being honest), and unaware of or unconcerned about other people's feelings. She will say and do things intentionally to try to hurt your feelings and push your buttons, but it is important to try to stay calm in those situations.

Don't allow yourself to get sucked into arguments. You don't have to attend every fight you're invited to. I met an older man with kids that were in their 30s. He told me he had never had a fight with his kids. In disbelief, I asked how that was possible, and he replied, "Fights require two people. I've been yelled at many times, but I didn't allow that to dictate my response and engage in a fight." He is a better man than me, but he is right. Staying calm by taking a deep breath, quoting scripture in your head, or repeating a mantra and not allowing yourself to drop to her level is one of the best things you can do when she is acting out.

STEP #3
Search for the root.

We know she doesn't slam the door because it's fun and she likes the sound. Most of the time we know the situation that caused her to act out, but many times we fail to get to the root of the issue. I recently took a silent car ride with one of my daughters where I repeatedly said, "Please just talk to me," and got nothing in return. I wanted to know what I had done wrong so I could apologize and hopefully fix it. It turned out that what I had done—not bringing her jacket to her after practice even though it was cold—was not the actual issue she was dealing with. When we got home, my wife, dealing with the situation much better than I had, discovered she was feeling overlooked because of something her teacher had done earlier that day, which was followed up by something her friend had done after school, and me not seeing her need had tipped the scales.

There is almost always a deeper root cause behind the action, attitude, or outburst. Seek to find that root by asking questions, looking critically at the situation, and being persistent in loving her through her behavior to get to the bottom of it.

STEP #4
Connect and listen.

It is not fun when your child is acting out, but it is a real opportunity to listen to her and build connection on a deeper level. Making up after an argument, letting her cry with you after she tells you what the rude girls at school said, or sitting quietly with her while she processes her emotions all build a deeper connection. Most of the time, a meltdown is a cry for the connection she is longing for. In these situations, it is easy to turn instantly to punishment or distance yourself from her, but in actuality, that only makes the disconnection worse.

Listen to her, be there for her, help her find a solution, and use the situation to build a connection with her.

STEP #5
Get support where needed.

"I need help." These are some of the hardest words you will ever speak, but sometimes it's exactly what you need to say. It is okay to ask for help. As parents, we think it's all on us, but part of that is doing what it takes to get what your daughter needs. Asking a friend, pastor, counselor, or doctor for help is not a sign of weakness; it is a sign of strength and dedication to your daughter. Get what you need so you can give her what she needs.

STEP #6
Lean on your faith.

Your daughter's outbursts can be crushing. I have lain awake many nights replaying conversations, worrying about situations, and wondering if my daughter will come out the other side all right. This is where we have to remind ourselves of Deuteronomy 31:8: "The Lord himself goes before you and will be with you; he will never leave you nor forsake you. Do not be afraid; do not be discouraged." Pray, read His Word, lean into his promises, and rest in your faith, and your God will get you—and your daughter—through these difficulties.

FOR REFLECTION

1. What are some things you can do to stay calm when your daughter is acting out?

2. Do you usually search for the root of the issue or just deal with what you see? How can you take a step to search for and deal with the root of the issue?

3. What are some ways you can be a better listener and use that to make stronger connections with your daughter?

4. How can your faith help you when your daughter is acting out? How can you better lean on God during those times?